THE *American Voice*

ANTHOLOGY

OF

POETRY

EDITED BY

FREDERICK SMOCK

THE UNIVERSITY PRESS OF KENTUCKY

Publication of this volume was made possible in part
by grants from the Kentucky Foundation for Women, Inc.,
and the National Endowment for the Humanities.

Scholarly publisher for the Commonwealth,
serving Bellarmine College, Berea College, Centre
College of Kentucky, Eastern Kentucky University,
The Filson Club Historical Society, Georgetown College,
Kentucky Historical Society, Kentucky State University,
Morehead State University, Murray State University,
Northern Kentucky University, Transylvania University,
University of Kentucky, University of Louisville,
and Western Kentucky University.

Editorial and Sales Offices: The University Press of Kentucky
663 South Limestone Street, Lexington, Kentucky 40508-4008

02 01 00 99 98   5 4 3 2 1

Library of Congress Cataloging-in-Publication Data

The American Voice anthology of poetry / edited by Frederick Smock.
        p. cm.
    ISBN 0-8131-2097-7 (alk. paper)–ISBN 0-8131-0956-6 (pbk. : alk. paper)
    1. Poetry–Collections. I. Smock, Frederick. II. American Voice
(Louisville, Ky.)
PN6101.A45 1998
811'.5408–dc21   98-14037
Cover illustration by Erica Kirchner.
This book is printed on acid-free recycled paper
meeting the requirements of the American National Standard
for Permanence of Paper for Printed Library Materials.

Manufactured in the United States of America

The American Voice Anthology of Poetry

Preface

In the fall of 1978, I left graduate school at the University of Arizona and moved back home to Kentucky. My decision had more to do with landscape, probably, than with academics. I took a part-time teaching job at the University of Louisville, where, by a happy circumstance, I was assigned to share a carrel with another part-timer, the writer Sallie Bingham.

Sallie had just moved back to Kentucky from New York City. We were both somewhat disconsolate, I suppose, each in our own way, and some of that surely came through in our first conversations, though we were too circumspect and probably too shy to confess it to one another. We talked about books and authors, and, through them, our own confounded destinies. We were both writing, too, Sallie with more success than I, and we talked about these delights and difficulties as well.

When we began to talk about making a literary journal, we first thought of calling it "Other Voices," to represent the Latin Americans, regionalists, women, and other minority writers we liked ~ that whole sudden explosion of voices, in the late '70s and early '80s, which were not finding publication within the literary establishment. One evening, our friend Frank MacShane suggested we locate the journal more centrally by calling it "The American Voice," or something similar. Once remarked, it seemed the obvious choice, and we adopted it immediately. In a subsequent letter, Frank wrote, "I am glad I had the wit to come up with the name. It establishes you without doubt or qualification, and that seems a good thing."

Sallie became the publisher, with me as her editor, and our first issue came out in the fall of 1984, with work from Marge Piercy, Leon Rooke, Sergio Ramírez (who was the vice-president of Nicaragua at the time), Bette Howland, Joe Ashby Porter, Ai, Michael Blumenthal, Anne Valley Fox, Fenton Johnson, and Elaine Equi, among others. A diverse lot. Our second issue featured Wendell Berry, Ernesto Cardenal, Jorge Luis Borges, Harrop A. Freeman, Jamake Highwater, Bienvenido Santos, Brenda Marie Osbey, et cetera. Since then, we have published hundreds of writers, many for the first time, from all the Americas ~ in the process, I hope, recovering a part of that beautiful and various name "America" from the political ideologues.

We have been guided by an abiding love for these other voices, for these frequently dissenting voices, and by our own desire to give them a forum at the center of the culture.

The vital edge of American publishing has always been located in the hinterlands, on the frontiers *within* our borders. In small, out-of-the-way places, in small journals and presses, our nation's literature is constantly being created. (Commercial publishers are the last to recognize serious talent.) Sallie and I have been lucky to be located away from the centers of traditional publishing power, where the engines of commerce drown out all but the loudest voices. Here, in the country, one can hear the leaves of grass singing.

A bit of local history: Thomas Merton (who published his own literary journal, *Monks Pond,* at Gethsemani) came to a mystical belief that Kentucky is the center of the universe. And, in point of curious fact, when Thomas Jefferson divided the old Northwest Territory into a grid of township squares, he first drew on his map a north-south meridian that began at the Falls of the Ohio, the portage where Louisville was founded; from this point would the New World begin. In some ways, and certainly by a coincidence of geography, we have been sharers in Jefferson's vision.

My goal in selecting poems that have first appeared in *The American Voice* is to create a balanced and representative collection. A collection that looks back and gathers up some of the more magical voices of our century ~ Jorge Luis Borges, Jane Cooper, James Still, May Swenson, Ruth Stone. Yet also a collection that looks to the future of poetry, with many younger poets whose best work, I hope, is still ahead of them. What place might Marilyn Chin, Mark Doty, Brigit Pegeen Kelly eventually assume in the pantheon?

The journal has been fortunate enough to have had works from its pages reprinted in *Pushcart Prize, Best American Poetry, Best American Essays,* and the *Breadloaf Anthology,* among other prize annuals, and, most significantly, to have won these recognitions for the work of emerging writers ~ Fae Myenne Ng, Susan Tichy, Kristina McGrath, Marie Sheppard Williams, Dennis Sampson, Suzanne Gardinier, Josie Foo, Robyn Selman, Nancy Mairs.

We have published some established authors, to be sure, but what does it mean to say that Muriel Rukeyser, for one example, is established, when none of her books is in print? This was the case as recently as a few years ago, until TriQuarterly and the Paris Press ~ both small presses ~ came to the rescue.

Because Sallie and I wanted a truly pan-American journal, we have relied on the help of many fine translators, and this anthology includes translations of Borges by Hardie St. Martin, Carmen Matute by Jo Anne Engelbert, Ernesto Cardenal by Jonathan Cohen, Pablo Antonio

Cuadra by Steven F. White, and Olga Orozco by Mary Crow. These and others, like Geoff Hargreaves, Norman Thomas di Giovanni, and Diana Decker, have provided not only translations but also the invaluable help of their advice, their spreading of the word.

Some inclusions in this volume may seem odd, for example, Odysseas Elytis, the Greek Nobel laureate. But we include him for the lovely translations of his poems into English by Greek-American poet Olga Broumas. Or the Israeli soldier/poet Yehuda Amichai, likewise for the translations into our language by Karen Alkalay-Gut. These poets, and some others, are of course well known far beyond the borders of this hemisphere. Some "regional" writers ~ like Richard Taylor, Sue Terry Driskell, Cia White ~ are scarcely known beyond the borders of Kentucky, yet they deserve a much wider audience.

I notice a great diversity, both stylistic and thematic, among these poems. And I am pleased that these poems do not tally up to any one definable editorial style, that there seems to be no typical *American Voice* poem. Each of these poems seems atypical, in its own special way, and therefore original and deserving of our closest reading.

To write or publish poems is to hold out some hope for the world, to contend mightily with the brutal politics of the marketplace, advertising, and the cheapening of the word. It is one interpretation, or application, of Dostoevsky's belief that we will be "saved" by beauty. Poems can be tough too, yet, though they may leave us shaken, they are also immeasurably generous. In this sense, then, are the poems in this anthology political, for any good writer's view of the world is necessarily subversive. But I hope these poems are also beautiful, and cast an enchanting light upon the reader.

~ Frederick Smock

Acknowledgments

I would like to thank Pat Buster, Ann Stewart Anderson, and Linda Watkins for their invaluable assistance. Thanks also to our contributing editors, Barbara Smith, Kristina McGrath, Marguerite Feitlowitz, Mark Doty and Marjorie Agosín, and to guest editors Aleda Shirley and Sarah Gorham.

And, finally, a special thanks to Sallie Bingham, who made it all happen.

The Text is Flesh

Paula Gunn Allen

They tell me that in Beirut
men lounge around the tables
over thick syrupy coffee
and recite poetry.

Not the ones they've made themselves,
but everyone's poems.
These are people who know
poems are word in flesh, incarnate.

In safer, more sterile worlds we sit
lounging over thin brown water
that steams, reciting formulas
about poems nobody read before.

Here, we are people who are not carnal.
Here, we do not hear the song flesh sings
on its way to death. Neither shadow
nor light are kenned.

In Beirut the bombs. Uzi and oud.
Rocket flares, explodes. Flesh splattered on walls.
Blood flows in cobbled alleys with all the filth,
among which in still courtyards oranges bloom.

Idiom is language of the heart.
I and thou and nowhere at all.
Ya babeebi, anine, ya babeebi.
Here over tiny cups a poem perches

on the edge of lips, stutters once;
talking breath feathers lift
winged flesh into sky
trembles into flight.

Conversations with the dead
convert energy to strength,
on the rez we talk such tales,
the ones who can talk, who know how.

A community of spirits,
kopisty'a, some in flesh,
some embodied words. A presence
don't you know. All in mind.

Feathered nests of minds. Such university, these cells,
these breathings, where wings of hair
flutter and fall to the ground. In Beirut
recitation, chanting. Uzi and oud,

carnal rotting, blood washing streets clean.
Life exploding into song,
chanting. Coffeehouses full of poetry,
courtyards full of blooms

flown and scattered, held,
passing back and forth, flower into flesh.
You know, *carnal.* Like that. *Tu es mi carnal,
mi carnales.* Flesh that is known.

In Beirut they chant together
stylized runes, incanted dreams.
Generations, thousands of them
around a table, chanting.

On the rez thunderheads, *shiwanna,*
mass around the mesas
chanting. We've watched them become
bolts of flame. Smokes of blast. The noise.

Seen them become rain. Bring at last the corn.
Here in fleshless luxury we imagine
they're in cause and effect relation.
On the rez and in Beirut we know it's not the same.

What there is, is text and earth.

What there is, is flesh.

And chanting flesh into death and life.

And somewhere within, exploding, some bone.

Oud is an Arabic stringed instrument like a guitar but with more
strings and a somewhat differently shaped body; its sound
differs from that of either an acoustical or electric guitar
(Arabic)

Ya babeebi, anine means I love you, light of my eye (Arabic)

Rez is modern American Indian slang for the reservation one
hails from

Kopisty'a means community or collectivity of spirits (Laguna
Pueblo: Keres)

Carnal means flesh, and intimate person, usually man to man
(Spanish)

Shiwanna means spirits who come as rainclouds (Laguna
Pueblo: Keres)

Incanted means having sacred power to create or enspell: related
to incantation

WHAT I LEARNED IN THE WARS

Yehuda Amichai

What did I learn in the wars:
To march in time to the swinging of arms and legs
like a pump pumping an empty well;
To march in procession and to be alone in the fray;
To bury myself in pillows and covers and the body of my
    beloved,
and to shout "Mother," without her hearing,
and to shout "God," without believing in Him —
and even if I did believe in Him
I would never tell Him about war
the way we keep from children their parents' atrocities.

What else did I learn? I learned to keep open an escape
    route:
Abroad, I take a room in a hotel
near the airport or train station,
and even in halls of rejoicing
always look for the little door
with EXIT written over it in red letters.

Battle too begins
like rhythmic dance drums, and its end
is "withdrawal with the dawn." Forbidden love
and battle both, at times, conclude this way.

But above all I learned the knowledge of camouflage,
so that I would not stand out, not be recognized,
so I would not be distinguishable from my surroundings,
even from my beloved,
so I would seem a bush, or a sheep,
a tree, a shadow of a tree.

a doubt, a shadow of a doubt,
an electrified fence, a dead stone,
a house, a cornerstone.

If I were a prophet I would dim the brilliance of vision
and black out my faith with black paper
and cover with netting my thoughts of divine chariots.

And when the time comes I'll put on the camouflage of my
    end:
the white of clouds and an expanse of sky blue
and endless stars.

Translated from the Hebrew
by Karen Alkalay-Gut

ONE OF US

Wendell Berry

Must another poor body, brought
to its rest at last, be made the occasion
of yet another sermon? Have we nothing
to say of the dead that is not
a dull mortal lesson to the living,
our praise of Heaven blunted
by this craven blaming of its earthly work?
We must go with the body to the dark
grave, and there at the edge turn back
together — it is all that we can do — remembering
her as she is now in our minds
forever: how she gathered the chicks
into her apron before the storm, and tossed
the turkey hen over the fence,
so that the little ones followed,
peeping, out of the tall grass, safe
from the lurking snake; how she was one
of us, here with us, who now is gone.

THE HEART OF QUANG DUC

Michael Blumenthal

Saigon, 11 June 1963

When Quang Duc poured gasoline all over his body
in the streets of Saigon in 1963
and lit a match to it,
there was a large conflagration, flames
shooting in all directions at once,
the flesh charring, then sizzling,
then almost disappearing into the fire
as his body's two hundred and seven bones,
its seventy percent that is water,
contracted towards ash. All of Quang Duc
had been reduced to rubble, except
for his heart, which, like a phoenix,
rose from the small bucket of ash intact
and was thought by his fellow Buddhists
to be an omen of all that survives
a mere man's death. Twice more
they lit the dead man's heart, hoping
to send it after him. Twice more
it would not burn, twice more it refused
to enters its master's dwelling,
as if to say: *not yet, not yet,*
I will not follow. But the third time
they poured fuel over the dead man's heart
and set it aflame, the heart joined itself
to the heat of that earlier fire, and,
like a pig's fat roasting on a spit,
sizzled into the afternoon, and was gone.
The Buddhists and Christians watched silently

as Quang Duc's heart sputtered into the air.
They knew they were learning something
that would serve them throughout the war —
that no man's heart
can survive more than three burnings,
that nothing can beat through fire
forever, or for very long.

ONE OF LEE'S SOLDIERS

Jorge Luis Borges

(1862)

A bullet has caught up with him on the bank
Of a clear river whose name he doesn't even know.
He pitches forward on his face. (This is a true
Story and the man is more than one man.)
The golden air stirs the lazy leaves
In the pine groves. A persevering ant
Clambers up on the indifferent face.
The sun climbs. Many things have changed
And will forever go on changing until
One day in the future when I sing
Of you who, without benefit of tears,
Dropped: a dead man.
No marble keeps track of your name,
Six feet of dirt are your obscure glory.

Translated from the Spanish
by Hardie St. Martin

LABORARE EST ORARE

Diana Brebner

I haven't forgotten all those fearful years
when work was prayer. There was nothing to

hope for in all that torture, but there I was
hoping for something to save me. He came so

close to killing me. And I kept telling myself
how much he loved me. What did I know about

love? Even then, I could strip old pine floors,
bake bread, plant those gardens which sustained

me. Bury another child. Go through all the
motions of making things work. Is prayer ever

only for believers? I came so close to finding
my own murder as an answer. Now, here is

this world I have worked so hard for. This
earth is no heaven, but it has its places where

I can find peace. Love, when I think of you,
there is never enough work to love you within,
there is never enough prayer.

This is such radiant life, and I am thankful:
Laborare est orare. Work is prayer.

Sacred Heart

Lee Ellen Briccetti

Even as a girl I knew the heart was not a valentine;
it was wet, like a leopard frog on a lily pad;
like a lily pad it had long tube roots

anchoring it in place.
And smaller roots too, like the lupine and marigold
and bleeding hearts' roots I traced with my finger

while transplanting in the garden.
I believed Jesus had a thousand bloody hearts
planted in our flowerbeds beneath the pink flowers;

they could see us through the ground.
I had a book about a girl who lived in the earth
near the tree roots, who cut off her finger

and used it as a key. I wondered if I could love like that.
I studied the painting of His chest peeled back
to show light around the Sacred Heart.

And in the bedroom at my grandmother's where I slept
against the tree shadows, I was the spirit
inside the room's heart, and my life was inside me

like something that could leave quietly through the window.

EVENSONG

Olga Broumas

The silvery leaf of insouciance lifts off the bay past dusk
and with it, like breath
or the barely visible exhaust
preceding nuclear explosion, dazzling,

the sand shifts deep below the house.
I feel its tremor in my ear, pillowed
on the futon on the floor,
and through it other tremors,

South Africa, Lebanon, the lower
American continent whose beauty and bounty
enervate our ghetto-bound conscience.
I float on my freedom my sleepless nights.

The bay, underhem
of our planet, link to my natal beach, blue algeous pinafore
home to whale and fleet,
no longer rests me. On it, the spit

of the Arab touches me,
the venom of the dispossessed inoculates me,
the vomit and sweat of the detained, soaked
into earth and filtered through it,

tenderly meet the fine white sand
as if what remained of suffering to speak
were love. I am held
in the field of my freedom,

for which I exiled myself as soon as I could,
blind as though a corneal membrane,
which I coiled all my life behind to break,
let in only intensities of dark and light,

and freedom was light shattering
the mesmer of high noon in the Aegean.
Held there, my body weeps,
meets these marine broadcasts with a sadness,

dry, spasmodic,
elusive of CAT scans and sleeping pills.
By day, I ask of those who come to me for answers,
what would you say, asked by a poet

whose tongue and nails have been removed, whose nipples
are cratered with ash, to account for your freedom?
Seize it! I urge,
and return by night to my seizures. Peace and serenity

are the temple I shape, whose officiate,
joy, is choking.
Some may be seen beating her
on the back with clubs, others

with tubes down her nose enjoin her to vigor.
The beauty of strawberries,
organic and hand-picked by my neighbor,
in the blue bowl by the open window under circling gulls,

is likewise insufficient to rouse this Demeter from her bane.
Daily I make my offerings,
nightly receive the clash of the objectors,
those who squeeze tissue salts from humans for their brine.

Like a pit in the fruit's ripe stomach,
encircled by airborne toxins clouding its permeable skin,
I am nourished, gratefully,
by the force of an unconditional

habit still linking life to the pulp of fruit.
Gestures of offering, smooth forearms of receiving,
between them the vivid colors of rare untainted food,
like a brooch with its gem,

are the medals we're known by and carry, how long,
into disarmament, to joy's free breath again above our heads.

FIXING THE BARN

Joseph Bruchac

for Robert Morgan

The old barn, five generations
in the family, had begun
to bow out at the west like an
old man's belly, the sway of wind
and drift of snow unsettling
a foundation laid only of
logs on flat stones pressed into soil.

The peak of the roof is a good
thirty feet above the hay mows,
stalls which held cows and work horses
whose names went back into the earth
of the old upper field with their
bones, when that day came when each step
was pain to them. Then Jesse dug
the hole, a morning's work, and walked
them to its edge. His whisper in
their left ears was the last praise heard
before the deep thunder of sleep.

Now only old tools, boxes, dust,
the crumble of hay under foot
remind one what this place once was.
Stored furniture lies under cloth
laid like layers of earth above
an ancient city of ancestors.

But it's not time to let this barn
go back into earth, its oak beams
are strong enough to outlast us.

The timbers, drilled for hand-carved pegs,
bend nail and thumb-thick spike alike.
High up in the rafters, we sweat
each link of the chain, cranking back
the sides to true, levelling up
the dip in timbers, tree-trunk thick,
which lie above the Great Field door.

When we are done, the new pine beams
shine bright, bracing the old brown wood,
joining the way our dreams tonight
link to a remembering rhythm,
the flow of muscle and grain through
all our five generations.

WOMAN IRONING

Olga Cabral

I am ironing the dress in which I ran from the prom
I am ironing my favorite dresses of long ago
I am ironing the dresses I did not have
and the ones that I did have, stitched so finely of fog
I am ironing the dress of water in which I met you
I am ironing our tablecloth of sun and our coverlet
    of moon
I am ironing the sky
I am folding the clouds like linen
I am ironing smoke

I am ironing sad foreheads and deep wrinkles of despair
I am ironing sackcloth
I am ironing bandages
I am ironing huge damp piles of worries
I am smoothing and patting and folding and hanging over
    chairs to air out and dry
I am ironing the tiniest things but for whom or for what
    I cannot imagine
I am ironing my shadow which is ironing me.

"FOR THOSE DEAD, OUR DEAD. . ."

Ernesto Cardenal

When you get the nomination, the award, the promotion,
think about the ones who died.
When you are at the reception, on the delegation, on the
    commission,
think about the ones who died.
When you have won the vote, and the crowd congratu-
    lates you,
think about the ones who died.
When you're cheered as you go up to the speaker's plat-
    form with the leaders,
think about the ones who died.
When you're welcomed by friends at the airport in the big
    city,
think about the ones who died.
When you're speaking into the microphone, when the tv
    cameras focus on you,
think about the ones who died.
When you become the one who gives out the certificates,
    orders, permission,
think about the ones who died.
When the little old lady comes to you with her problem,
    some little matter,
think about the ones who died.
                See them without shirts on, degraded,
            gushing blood, wearing hoods, blown up,
arranged in piles, shafted, their eyes gouged out,
                beheaded, riddled with bullets,
            dumped along the side of the road,
                in holes they dug themselves,
                    in communal graves,

or just lying on the ground, enriching the soil of mountain
    plants:
You represent them.
The ones who died
delegated you.

Translated from the Spanish by
Jonathan Cohen

The Long Way Around

Barbara Carey

not that door!
he said, it's locked
after dark

& directed me
the long way around

all along
the high glimmer
of windows

(history was inside)

& me, at this late hour
rattling the handle
of every possibility

which will spring open?

THE WEEK

Richard Chess

Now in its sixth day, like a pear it has swelled
to a ripeness nearly beyond belief.
Already this week he has blessed a bread
baked by a man whose testicles have been eaten by cancer,
already he has heard a Bat Mitzvah student
like an angel sing Isaiah
while waiting outside his study door.
This morning he pulls the blue shirt
from the closet and now, *tefillin*
snaked around his arm, begins to sway.
Does he pray for the brick by brick rebuilding
of the Temple,
or for the hour when children to their parents will turn
like tiger to lamb,
or for his wife, eating her egg?
In a few hours she will arrive at the clinic, quietly
cross the sacred line picketers make, and sign
in for the abortion. She is not ready
for a child.
She scours the pan to a reflecting finish, hesitates
at the still sink, and notices
through the window a cardinal in the yard.
Upstairs he sings, a rabbi out of key,
carried away on a skin of light, shaking
his free hand at the sun.

AUTUMN LEAVES

Marilyn Chin

The dead piled up, thick, fragrant, on the fire-escape.
My mother ordered me again, and again, to sweep it clean.
All which blooms must fall. I learned this not from the Tao,
    but from high school biology.

Oh, the contradictions of having a broom and not a dustpan!
I swept the leaves down, down through the iron grille
and let the dead rain over the Wong family's patio.

And it was Achilles Wong who completed the task.
    We called her:
The-one-who-cleared-away-another-family's-autumn.
She blossomed, tall, benevolent, notwithstanding.

LADY OF THE HAYSTACK

Jennifer Clement

Strange abacist,
She'd count pebbles and count
The flecks, specks, and particles
Of her grass nursery.
She knew all
That dwelled in her damp berth,
Thick with ants,
It was an atlas
Of cobwebs, thistle-down,
The tiniest mushrooms
And weed.

On brumal, frosty nights,
Through the yellow-mustard hay,
She'd add and subtract meteors,
Comets, shooting stars,
Blue fireflies,
And fill her
Twisted sorrow
With numbers.

And later, years later,
At the stark,
Black-box asylum,
She'd count her strands of hair,
And stand only by windows.
Still,
Her breath smelled grainy
Of all the earth's dark sediments.
And the other melancholy
Madwomen

Sheltered near her
For the sugar
Sweet hay scent
Of her arms.

The Lady of the Haystack made her appearance in 1776 near Bristol. She lived for four years in a haystack before being moved to an asylum.

FOR A BIRTHDAY

Jane Cooper

Something is dragging me backward
to my fifth year
when I began my quarrel with God.

I step into the morning
after the first frost —

The beeches are radiant,
shaking their bones clothed in honey,
shivering in delicious fear.

If only we too turned golden
at the first stroke of cold.

I shall walk by the river in the sun,
studying transparency
and the book of impersonal love.

POEM OF THE FOREIGNERS' MOMENT IN OUR JUNGLE

Pablo Antonio Cuadra

(for several voices)

In the heart of our mountains, where the old jungle
devours roads the way the *guás* eats snakes,
where Nicaragua raises its flag of blazing rivers
    among torrential drums...
There, long before my song,
even before I existed, I invent the stone called flint
and I ignite the sordid green of *heliconias,*
the mangroves' boiling silence,
and I set fire to the orchid in the boa constrictor's night.
I cry out. Scream. Star! Who just opened the night's doors?
I must make something from the mud of history,
dig down in the swamp and unearth the moons
of my forefathers. Oh, unleash
your dark rage, magnetic snake,
sharpen your obsidian claws, black tiger, stare
with your phosphorescent eyes, there!
    In the heart of the jungle,
    500 North Americans!

They're marching,
singing among the *sotocaballos* and the *ñámbaros,*
singing to the rhythm of their marching feet.
And Nicaragua's last moons plummet from treetops.
(Red *lapas* chatter in crazy tongues.)

In the heart of our mountains, 500 Marines with machine-
    guns make their way.

    I hear voices,

slender swords of fever.

Anopheles.

Vulgar eagles from their tiny, trampled coins

e pluribus unum

"Ah!"

    We witness

the frenzied retreat of 500 North Americans,

defeated and pale,

their blood burned by the last flames of Acripeña's
    farm,

trembling with the cold of Andrés Regules' death,

the cold of Orlando Temolián's death,

Fermín Maguel's (all miskito Indians).

500 fleeing North Americans,

with malaria,

their footprints lost from swamp to swamp,

delirious,

Túngula

Túngula

The great frog leaps, my friend.

The rain calls once again.

I hear voices: the blue spiders

weave a new virgin flag.

Before my song,

even before I existed,

in the heart of our mountains,

beneath the sordid green of *heliconias,*

beneath the mangroves' boiling silence,

I invent the stone called flint

and I ignite their white bones delicately polished
    by the ants.

                    (Alamicamba)

                    Translated from the Spanish
                        by Steven F. White

BROADWAY

Mark Doty

Under Grand Central's tattered vault
— maybe half a dozen electric stars
still lit — one saxophone blew,

and a sheer black scrim billowed
over some minor constellation
under repair. Then, red wings

in a storefront tableau, lustrous,
the live macaws preening, beaks
opening and closing like those

animated knives that unfold all night
in jewelers' windows. For sale,
glass eyes turned out towards the rain,

the birds lined up like the endless flowers
and cheap gems, the makeshift tables
of secondhand magazines and shoes

the hawkers eye while they shelter
in the doorways of banks. So many
pockets and paper cups and hands

reeled over the weight of that
glittered pavement, and at 103rd
and Broadway a woman reached to me

across the wet roof of a stranger's car
and said, *I'm Carlotta, I'm hungry.*
She was only asking for change,

so I don't know why I took her hand.
The rooftops were glowing above us,
enormous, crystalline, a second city

lit from within. That night a man
on the downtown local stood up
and said, *My name is Ezekiel,*

I am a poet, and my poem this evening
is called "Fall." He held himself
straight to recite, a child

reminded of his posture
by the gravity of his text, his hands
hidden in the pockets of his coat.

Love is protected, he said,
the way leaves are packed in snow,
the rubies of fall. God is protecting

the jewel of love for us. He didn't ask
for anything, but I gave him
all the change left in my pocket,

and the man beside me, impulsive,
moved, gave Ezekiel his watch.
It wasn't an expensive watch.

I don't even know if it worked,
but the poet started, then rushed
as if so much good fortune must be

hurried away from, before anyone
realizes it's a mistake. Carlotta,
her stocking cap glazed

like feathers in the rain,
under the radiant towers,
the floodlit ramparts,

must have wondered at my impulse
to touch her, which was like touching
myself, the way your own hand feels

when you hold it because you want
to feel contained. She said,
You get home safe now, you hear?

In the same way, Ezekiel turned back
to the benevolent stranger.
I will write a poem for you tomorrow,

he said. *The poem I will write
will go like this: Our ancestors
are replenishing the jewel of love for us.*

— *for Jean Valentine*

So Much of My Garden Is Iris

Sue Terry Driskell

I can tell a long time ahead
which Siberian iris will flower.
Probably none where they have been thinned,
moved to a new plot.
They don't like to be pulled apart.

The pencil-thin leaf
turns from green to lavender.
Flower stalks shoot high, buds thicken,
purple tips enlarge,
emerge from lavender leaves.

Then I'll walk into the garden
and all the iris will be blooming at once,
displaying three petals, their throats
touched by fine white lines,
like lines of pain around your eyes
those last days.

              In less than a week
the beauty will shrivel, curl inward.

ANOINT THE ARISTON

Odysseas Elytis

VIII.

Naked, July, high noon. In a narrow bed, between rough cambric sheets, cheek on my arm I lick and taste its salt. I look at the whitewash on the wall of my small room. A little higher is the ceiling with the beams. Lower, the trunk where I have set all my belongings: two pairs of pants, four shirts, white underclothes. Next to them, the chair with the huge matting. On the floor, on the white and black tiles, my two sandals. I have by my side also a book.

I was born to have so much. Paradox doesn't interest me. From the least you get anywhere faster. Only it is more difficult. You can get there from the girl you love as well, but you must know to touch her only when nature obeys you. And from nature too — but you must know to remove her thorn.

IX.

"Yesterday I thrust my hand under the sand and touched hers. All afternoon then the geraniums looked at me from the courtyards with meaning. The boats, the ones pulled out to land, took on something known, familiar. And at night, late, when I removed her earrings to kiss her as I want to, with my back against the stone church wall, the pelago thundered and the Saints came out holding candles to give me light."

Without doubt there is for each of us a separate, uncontrovertible sensation which if we don't find and isolate in time, and cohabit with later, and fill with visible acts, we're lost.

X.

Whatever I was able to acquire in my life by way of acts visible to all, that is, to win my own transparency, I owe it to a kind of special courage Poetry gave me: to become wind for the kite and kite for the wind, even when the sky is missing. I'm not playing with words. I'm talking about the motion one discovers signing itself inside the "moment," when one can open it and make it last. When, in fact, Sorrow becomes Grace and Grace Angel; Joy Alone and Sister Joy

with white, long pleats over the void,

a void full of bird's condensation, basil breezes and hissings of an echoing Paradise.

Translated from the Greek
by Olga Broumas

PURITANS

Elaine Equi

There are no small ones.
All big boned

men and women
without a hint of child's play.

They creak
as they walk

like doors left open
to bang in the wind.

One imagines from their gait
that years from now

they will make adroit bowlers.
Meanwhile, they whisper

careful not to sound rhythmic.
Dovegray, lavender and eggshell

are the only colors
and even these must be bleached, muted,

in order for their profiles
to emerge on cold cash

as if doodled there
with invisible ink.

If not optimistic,
they are eternally democratic

and can be handled
without "contamination."

That word
has no meaning for them.

Touch them
as much as you like,

wherever you please.
They have never felt

the desire to reciprocate
and for that they are grateful.

GRAVITY

Jan Freeman

The outer petals of the champagne rose
brown, stiffen, and retreat from the bud's softness.
The sky is more bitter than bright;
sister, it is our one acrid reminder:
the blood under our skin
blue above our heads.

Permeable, the tongue searches for its likeness;
flammable, the heart attempts the same but knows better.
This is not a game of evasion or invention
or even passion.
It is the arch digging for a nesting place.
It is the importance of the roof.
It is the catechism of balance versus the catechism
    of imbalance.
It is the posture necessary to right myself,
the sentient knowledge of fingertips.
It is the mother of light
and the daughter of darkness.

This room is a fossil equipped to steal imprints:
breasts, thighs, mouth, arms, neck.
Voices of escapees cool my palms.
I am the pitiful woman whose silence is stronger
than the walls of any house,
whose mind and body battle each other to impotence.

I am not a marrying ground.
I am not a nursing ground.
Do not call me miss.
Do not call me mama.

Do not beg for blessings.
I am like and unlike.
My mouth shuts easily,
but I have a word for every opening and every open space.

Lift the door and the way out alters the body's
    comprehension.
Thorns try to trap;
offspring sink to the bottom of the weeping wells;
but here we have dropped our own spirits into a pot,
here they have been clarified.
The bone rooms on the other side remain constantly
    jammed;
but in this small space even the unnamed and the
    unknown are protected.
Here we are as safe as the serpent used to be.

The language reaches far past absence,
past the fossils and the silence,
back to the sack and the spill,
to the moment of water,
to the time of the palm and the roof.
The fists forget themselves.
There is only the spray, the sticks, the hands, the scent of
    the sea at night;
the beautiful body stretches open, tunnels far into dark-
    ness, and then rises
to cut plainly the shoreline and the skyline.

Here the dead petals split from the heart are wings.
Our bodies provide balance:
we are flight;
we are our own grounding.
We have come to the place without the serpent.
The hands wrung tight as linen open.
Stand quiet for a moment.
Listen as the words of the bone rooms
gasp on the cold stone floor.

Listen as a few of the stubborn hearts alter.
Listen to the fear run out;
soon it will only be memory.

LYNX LIGHT

Tess Gallagher

The quilt has slipped
my shoulders. Let's be two sluggish fires
who say: winter
has again taught us something — speak
or be silent.

It is as if a lynx coexists with a housecat
when you kiss the knots in my fate
like that. Give me winter for constancy
and looking back: most silent because
most decided. Teach me
how to shed this cold devotion
by which memory
is exchanged for alertness.

Come and go
with me
like the sickle of a black tail
through a transparent net of birdsong.

WHERE BLIND SORROW IS TAUGHT TO SEE

Suzanne Gardinier

1

Rain shines black where the red-and-white-light-laced
street divides and becomes two The walkers
hunch coats over their heads but no rain falls
here Humming the wall between us is your voice
you who give me shelter for the night
Foot to piston fire to axle to tire
to street with rain between makes music
surge and ebb with each change of light This
song finds your window across our bridge
you who shelter me for the night
When does a bridge connect and when
divide When the wind pushes further in
to this room the sill glistens Chimes ring but
softly Your laugh rises and hushes them
you who give me shelter for the night
Sirens slur their frantic words but here
there is no danger The buttons down my shirt
have all day held in my loneliness
I unfasten them invisible
to you who give me shelter for the night
The light on the page fails just outside
the window The sheets are cool and dry
The street slicks and chills split in two Your warm
arpeggios sound through the lath and plaster
you who give me shelter for the night.

2

It's Independence Day or by now
Independence Night I have waited for you
so long The day's heat rises from the streets
but the light wind comes if we pull the curtains
aside Show me everything We will have
our own speeches and our own processions
our own declarations our own pageants
of union But there will be no banners
and no militia Heard around the world
will be only this Each part of your body
is speaking a different language scapula
clavicle nipples hard and soft against
my lips Within each language are hundreds
of dialects slangs speech rhythms and
impediments within each of these millions
of tones of human voice and inflection
My only hope of being able
to understand even the smallest part
of the conversation is to draw as close
as I can I turn you on your side
and run my tongue from the small of your back
down slowly over every province
between there and your navel on the other side
and back again and again and again
I listen I circumnavigate the world

MY MOTHER'S CLOTHES

Jane Gentry

On a December night
I brought them
from her nursing home,
and forgot them on the porch
under stars brittle with cold.
I left them hanging, far
from the warmth
of her body, away from fires
that keep the winter from us.
Her clothes, familiar to me
as her skin: the wool plaid
dress she made; her favorite
jacket, hunter green,
with its lapel pin, DWG,
my father gave her;
the shape of the body
holding as they swung
from their shoulders
on the porch, arms empty
against the weather.

SONNET FOR THE LAST EMPRESS OF CHINA

Sarah Gorham

THE EMPRESS'S DWARF APRICOT

At every joint another needle of green.
She prunes to fit the oval
table — new buds, the fleshy main
tuber. Now let the auxiliary root system
take over, furrow deep into black soil.
Its hidden rhizomes are like dangling
tongues, for desire burns low when contained
but burns nevertheless. Prune again
and it turns to concentrate, gunpowder
strong. She staggers up, dizzied
by too much stooping, the rush
of blood to her brain. With her headdress
and sinewy neck, she looks top heavy.
Tiny tree, burdened by its flowers.

BY THE WATERS OF BABYLON

E. J. Graff

A child lies looking at the ceiling, practicing
the unfamiliar language of prayers.
Where is my father? Here is my father, she says
and says again in past tense, in future tense, unconditionally,
in that language that her father cannot understand.
And it was evening, and it was morning, she says,
thinking from right to left, until
God rests, and she starts again.
And in the morning she will be the best speller ever,
her hand bobbing, over and over, above the rest of the class
with the earnestness of the drowned.

And in her thirteenth year the prayerbooks open
to her mother fasting in her narrow body, eyes closed,
to her father whispering jokes in the child's ear,
his leg so strong against hers that she trembles, saying
Blessed art thou oh Lord our God, King of the Universe,
who has commanded us, who has brought us to this day.
And when the congregation rises to daven, silently reciting
Forgive us for the sins we do not know we have committed,
already she is stumbling into exile,
into a body whose language she cannot understand,
and which her father will not touch, averting his eyes.

AGAINST ELEGIES

Marilyn Hacker

James has cancer. Catherine has cancer.
Melvin has AIDS.
Whom will I call, and get no answer?
My old friends, my new friends who *are* old,
or older, sixty, seventy, take pills
before or after dinner. Arthritis
scourges them. But irremediable night is
farther away from them; they seem to hold
it at bay better than the young-middle-aged
whom something, or another something, kills
before the chapter's finished, the play staged.
The curtains stay down when the light fades.

Morose, unanswerable, the list
of thirty- and forty-year-old suicides
(friends' lovers, friends' daughters) insists
in its lengthening: something's wrong.
The sixty-five-year-olds are splendid, vying
with each other in work-hours and wit.
They bring their generosity along,
setting the tone, or not giving a shit.
How well, or how eccentrically, they dress!
Their anecdotes are to the point, or wide
enough to make room for discrepancies.
But their children are dying.

Natalie died by gas in Montpeyroux.
In San Francisco, Ralph died
of lung cancer, AIDS years later, Lew
wrote to me. Lew, who, at forty-five,
expected to be dead of drink, who, ten

years on, wasn't, instead survived
a gentle, bright, impatient younger man.
(Cliché: he falls in love with younger men.)
Natalie's father came, and Natalie,
as if she never had been there, was gone.
Michèle closed up their house (where she
was born). She shrouded every glass inside

— mirrors, photographs — with sheets, as Jews
do, though she's not a Jew.
James knows, he thinks, as much as he wants to.
He's been working half-time since November.
They made the diagnosis in July.
Catherine is back in radiotherapy.
Her schoolboy haircut, prematurely grey,
now frames a face aging with other numbers:
"stage two," "stage three" mean more than "fifty-one"
and mean, precisely, nothing, which is why
she stares at nothing: lawn chair, stone,
bird, leaf; brusquely turns off the news.

I hope they will be sixty in ten years
and know I used their names
as flares in a polluted atmosphere,
as private reasons where reason obtains
no quarter. Children in the streets
still die in grandfathers' good wars.
Pregnant women with AIDS, schoolgirls, crack whores,
die faster than men do, in more pain,
are more likely than men to die alone.
What are our statistics, when I meet
the lump in my breast, you phone
the doctor to see if your test results came?

The earth-black woman in the bed beside
Lidia on the AIDS floor — deaf and blind:
I want to know if, no, how, she died.
The husband, who'd stopped visiting, returned?

He brought the little boy, those nursery-
school smiles taped on the walls? She traced
her name on Lidia's face
when one of them needed something. She learned
some Braille that week. Most of the time, she slept.
Nobody knew the baby's HIV
status. Sleeping, awake, she wept.
And I left her name behind.

And Lidia, where's she
who got her act so clean
of rum and Salem Filters and cocaine
after her passing husband passed it on?
As soon as she knew
she phoned and told her mother she had AIDS
but no, she wouldn't come back to San Juan.
Sipping *café con leche* with dessert,
in a blue robe, thick hair in braids,
she beamed: her life was on the right
track, now. But the cysts hurt
too much to sleep through the night.

No one was promised a shapely life
ending in a tutelary vision.
No one was promised: if
you're a genuinely irreplaceable
grandmother or editor
you will not need to be replaced.
When I die, the death I face
will more than likely be illogical:
Alzheimer's or a milk truck: the absurd.
The Talmud teaches we become impure
when we die, profane dirt, once the word
that spoke this life in us has been withdrawn,

the letter taken from the envelope.
If we believe the letter will be read,
some curiosity, some hope

come with knowing that we die.
But this was another century
in which we made death humanly obscene:
Soweto El Salvador Kurdistan
Armenia Shatila Baghdad Hanoi
Auschwitz Each one, unique as our lives are,
taints what's left with complicity,
makes everyone living a survivor
who will, or won't, bear witness for the dead.

I can only bear witness for my own
dead and dying, whom I've often failed:
unanswered letters, unattempted phone
calls, against these fictions. A fiction winds
her watch in sunlight, cancer ticking bone
to shards. A fiction looks
at proofs of a too-hastily finished book
that may be published before he goes blind.
The old, who tell good stories, half expect
that what's written in their chromosomes
will come true, that history won't interject
a virus or a siren or a sealed

train to where age is irrelevant.
The old rebbetzen at Ravensbruck
died in the most wrong place, at the wrong time.
What do the young know different?
No partisans are waiting in the woods
to welcome them. Siblings who stayed home
count down doom. Revolution became
a dinner party in a fast-food chain,
a vendetta for an abscessed crime,
a hard-on market for consumer goods.
A living man reads a dead woman's book.
She wrote it; then, he knows, she was turned in.

For every partisan
there are a million gratuitous

deaths from hunger, all-American
mass murders, small wars,
the old diseases and the new.
Who dies well? The privilege
of asking doesn't have to do with age.
For most of us
no question what our deaths, our lives, mean.
At the end, Catherine will know what she knew,
and James will, and Melvin,
and I, in no one's stories, as we are.

CAPE LIGHT

James Baker Hall

for Patricia Meyer Spacks

Various values for the size of the earth are current,
the great prize is still being offered,
schools have just let out,
others will be forming soon,

early summer, Cape Anne, from the screened porch.
You go to seven stores and climb over many chairs
to pick the one, an old dream, the favorite spot,

you cover it, the red blanket,
even a place to stack books,

then, day after day, don't sit in it.
Things keep happening in the outside world,

regret the common theme.
The sea rocks bear witness.
Do you remember the white wicker rocker,
the table with the glass top,

the children playing on the sloping yard,
above the water? Gravity

a property of the space itself,
the enigmatic rocks, light

rushing over them?
The black and white
birds?

DRUM

Linda Hogan

Inside the dark human waters
of our mothers,
inside the blue drum of skin
that beats the slow song of our tribes
we knew the drifts of continents
and moving tides.

We are the people who left water
to enter a dry world.
We have survived soldiers and drought,
survived hunger
and living
inside the unmapped terrain
of loneliness.
That is why we have thrust.
It is why
when we love
we remember our lives in water,
that other lives fall through us
like fish swimming in an endless sea,
that we are walking another way
than time
to new life, backwards
to deliver ourselves to rain and river,
this water
that will become other water
this blood that will become other blood
and is the oldest place
the deepest world
the skin of water
that knows the drum before a hand meets it.

ONE NOTE TOLLING

Lynda Hull

In the plaza, ornamental trees
remind the lieutenant of swan boats
he'd once seen on a green lake
when he was a boy. Here children splash
in the cracked fountain of Santa Maria

at the center of the square. Water
pours from the saint's hands
over their sleek dark heads.
He thought again of how the woman looked
last night before the interrogation

in her red shoes, the straight
chrome chair. This white-washed room
had blue tiles on the floor
her shoes had barely reached.
Her name was Consuelo. When he touched

the electrode to her temple, the skin
was like fine cream, unmarked by sun.
In a dim restaurant, the minister
of information had finished his meal.
Wine bottles glimmered, racked at the bar

like a row of shells. With a flourish
the waiter tore up the bill. The hills
and tall groves of eucalyptus flickered
with heat lightning. The woman clenched
her jaw and the cords of her neck

had seemed, almost, to lock. Then her voice
opened — one note tolling with the bells
from the convent above the city.

The curfew began. She called for a basin
of water. In June she had turned twenty.

In the restaurant, the waiter heard bells
as he swept the floor and stacked chairs.
She had a vision of herself floating
through high galleries, wearing
white, silence, the sky falling down

in wide bands across the floor
and there on the wall her sister's
painting had poured its colors out
into the emptiness: the jungle coast
and a squad of spider monkeys, their faces

cobalt and coral, and here, her own face
flaring in the green fire of branches.
The nuns of Santa Maria claimed a ribbon
of light fell from the sky, the third
that night. June was the month

of her brother's disappearance.
She said nothing. When the lieutenant
loosened his hand from her hair,
fists of it fell to the tiles. The first
heavy drops pocked the plaza's thick dust

and the nuns telling their beads said
the tears of the Virgin were raining.

A COURT PROPOSAL

Ha Jin

For centuries our kingdom has been harassed
by the barbarians, who can leave home with ease
and swiftly penetrate our frontier defense.
Why so? One obvious reason is that
there are no pretty women in the North.
So their men are tough and fierce.

Your Majesty, I propose we let them
have thousands of beauties.
These women will tie the savages
to their land—the men will be ensnared
and befuddled by feminine charm,
averse to the life on horseback.

We should teach their women footbinding
and open clothing shops in the prairie.
Gradually the men will learn to prize
feminine beauty—the willow waist,
the lily face, the lotus gait—
which will soften their harsh natures.

Thus their descendants will be civilized,
fond of books and shy of the spear.
Within three generations
they will be a part of us.

WINTER APPLES

Myrr Jonason

My son lay on his bed
with one cheek on the cold sill,
window open, visible eye rapt
watching the juniper, that cheek chapped
winter red. Mom. Mom. Hoarse voice
from under cover and only a foot twists
in the excitement of seeing—the birds—
and of not being seen. Mom. Mom.
I see them too then,
their red breasts jostling, packed
in juniper, the branches plunging
like censors: swinging fire
in brass pots. I hear the chain-clatter
of their calling, their gorge
on dust-blue berries, the blast,
ground splatter, gone—burst
of many birds. And I see too
my son, stirring now like one
who has seen, one who has heard.

THE MUSIC LESSON

Brigit Pegeen Kelly

Collect of white dusk. And
The first epistolary drops
Strike sparks from the leaves,

Send up the sweet fragrance
Of the Far Gone. Where
The maple fell in another rain

Red and white umbrellas
Hold back the weather: sun
And moon and the seasonal

Displays the four hands
Keep time to: the telling
And the told. Back and forth:

Back and forth: the lesson's
Passion is patience. Through
The domino tumble and clutter

Of the pupil's untutored touch
The metronome keeps
A stiff upper lip, pays out

Its narrow train of thought,
While above, God,
Gold carrion in a lit frame,

Rehearses His reproach, one-
Noted. Final. The unnegotiable
Real estate of absolute loss:

Discipleship's cost. O hands,
Hands, doing their work:
The steeple hat of the dunce

Is stiff with recalcitrant
Notes, but still the ghost hammers
Leap. And luck makes an entrance

In this: See: lightning
Partitions the dusk — illuminating
Our brief lease — and with

A cocksure infusion of heat
Luck lays hands on
The boy's hands and prefigures

The pleasure that will one day
Possess this picture for good.
This is the stone the builders

Rejected. Pleasure. *Pleasure.*
The liquid tool, the golden
Fossil that will come to fuel

In lavish and unspeakable ways
All the dry passages
The boy does not now comprehend

Or care for. And then his
Stricken hands will blossom
Fat with brag. And play.

AFTER THE HURRICANE

Jane Kenyon

I walk the fibrous woodland path to the pond.
Acorns break from the oaks, drop
through amber autumn air
which does not stir. The dog runs way ahead.

I find him snuffling on the shore
among water weeds that detached in the surge;
a broad, soft band of rufous pine needles;
a bar of sand, and shards of mica
glinting in the bright but tepid sun.

Here, really, we had only hard rain.
The cell I bought for the lamp
and kettles of water I drew remain
unused. All day we were restless, drowsy,
and afraid, and finally, let down:
we didn't get to demonstrate our grit.

In the full, still pond the likeness
of golden birch leaves and the light they emit
shines exact. When the dog sees himself
his hackles rise. I stir away his trouble
with a stick.

A crow breaks in upon our satisfaction.
We look up to see it lift heavily
from its nest high in the hemlock, and the bough
equivocate in the peculiar light. It was
the author of *Walden,* wasn't it,
who made a sacrament of saying *no.*

DEADLINE

Barbara Kingsolver

January 15, 1991

The night before war begins, and you are still here.
You can stand in a breathless cold
ocean of candles, a thousand issues of your same face
rubbed white from below by clear waxed light.
A vigil. You are wondering what it is
you can hold a candle to.

You have a daughter. Her cheeks curve
like aspects of the Mohammed's perfect pear.
She is three. Too young for candles but
you are here, this is war.
Flames covet the gold-sparked ends of her hair,
her nylon parka laughing in color,
inflammable. It has taken your whole self
to bring her undamaged to this moment,
and waiting in the desert at this moment
is a bomb that flings gasoline in a liquid sheet,
a laundress' snap overhead, wide as the ancient Tigris,
and ignites as it descends.

The polls have sung their opera of assent: the land
wants war. But here is another America,
candle-throated, sure as tide.
Whoever you are, you are also this granite anger.
In history you will be the vigilant dead
who stood in front of every war with old hearts
in your pockets, stood on the carcass of hope
listening for the thunder of its feathers.

The desert is diamond ice and only stars above us here
and elsewhere, a thousand issues of a clear waxed star,
a holocaust of heaven
and somewhere, a way out.

CAMOUFLAGING THE CHIMERA

Yusef Komunyakaa

We tied branches to our helmets.
We painted our faces & rifles
with mud from a riverbank,

with blades of grass hanging from the pockets
of our tiger suits. We wove
ourselves into the terrain,
content to be a hummingbird's target.

We hugged the tall grass & leaned
against a breeze off the river,
slowdragging with ghosts

from Saigon to Bangkok,
with women left in doorways
reaching in from America.
We aimed at dark-hearted songbirds.

In our waystation of shadows
rock apes tried to blow our cover,
throwing stones at the sunset. Chameleons

crawled our spines, changing from day
to night. Green to gold.
Gold to black. But we waited
till the moon touched metal,

till something almost broke
inside us. Like black silk
wrestling iron through the grass,

VC struggled with the hillside.
We weren't there. The river ran

through our bones. Small animals took refuge
against our bodies, as we held our breath,

ready to spring the L-shaped
ambush, as a world revolved
under each man's eyelid.

Persistent Heat

Natalie Kusz

They say beneath these fields, the soil
has burned for twenty years. A barley
farmer lit rags on a tractor, waited
to collect insurance. Those flames took
on half the village before they gathered
back and started down, eroding
through mosses, roots, dry leaves not
yet decayed into dirt. The seam
is still there: running miles under snow, kindling
earth like a geode sparkling
inside. They say when the fire surfaces, whole acres
fall in on themselves. When you walk these fields, go
gently, they say, feeling ahead
with each foot, gauging
what the ground can bear.

The Wandering Words

James Laughlin

This morning at breakfast, when I meant to say,
"Where's the marmalade?" my voice said instead,
"Where's the drawbridge?" and later
At the post office, when I handed my package slip
To Betty, the clerk, I asked her please to
Bring my strawberries. "Where would you get
Strawberries in December?" she asked as she
Brought me my package of books. You see, about
Six weeks before I'd had what the neurologist
Called a TIA, a little stroke. "Nothing
To worry about," he said. "It's normal
At your age. Take an aspirin a day and
It will go away." But it hasn't. Some wires
Must be crossed in the computer in my brain.
At first when the words began to wander
I was frightened. Was I going crazy?
Then I was annoyed. It was an embarrassment
With strangers to have to try to explain.
But now I think the wanderers are funny.
I wait with anticipation to hear what
Curious malapropism will pop out next.
I jot them down on a card I keep in my
Shirt pocket to see if there is a pattern.
I'm going to rearrange them into a poem,
A poem that may turn out to be
A surrealist masterpiece as good as
André Breton's *Soluble Fish*
Or his *Communicating Vases*.

APHASIA

Dorianne Laux

for Honeya

After the stroke all she could say
was Venezuela, pointing to the pitcher
with its bright blue rim, her one word
command. And when she drank the clear
water in and gave the glass back
it was Venezuela again, gratitude,
maybe, or the world now simply
a sigh, like the sky in the window,
the pillows a cloudy definition
propped beneath her head. Pink roses
dying on the bedside table, each fallen
petal a scrap in the shape of a country
she'd never been to, had never once
expressed interest in, and now
it was everywhere, in the peach
she lifted, dripping, to her lips,
the white tissue in the box, her brooding
children when they came to visit,
baptized with their new name
after each kiss. And at night
she whispered it, dark narcotic
in her husband's ear as he bent
to listen, her hands fumbling
at her buttons, her breasts,
holding them up to the light like a gift.
Venezuela, she said.

A STORY

Li-Young Lee

Sad is the man who is asked for a story
and can't come up with one.

His five-year-old son waits in his lap.
Not the same story, Baba. A new one.
The man rubs his chin, scratches his ear.

In a room full of books in a world
of stories, he can recall
not one, and soon, he thinks, the boy
will give up on his father.

Already the man lives far ahead, he sees
the day this boy will go. *Don't go!*
Hear the alligator story! The angel story once more!
You love the spider story. You laugh at the spider.
Let me tell it!

But the boy is packing his shirts,
he is looking for his keys. *Are you a god,*
the man screams, *that I sit mute before you?*
Am I a god that I should never disappoint?

But the boy is here. *Please, Baba, a story?*
It is an emotional rather than logical equation,
an earthly rather than heavenly one,
which posits that a boy's supplications
and a father's love add up to silence.

In that Desert

*written for the AIDS Wall
in Portland, 1989*

Ursula LeGuin

A lizard with no tail
looked at me and its flicked tongue
said: Belief in punishment
is punishment, belief
in sin is sin.

Its eye like a black stone
said: Love is punished
terribly. Belief
is a dry torrent.
The fire I die in
flickers my bright wings.

FOR ISHI

Sabra Loomis

Turtle thought he had made the world up
in the sleep of the old days.
He had thought it out
in his small head perfectly mounted,
eyes that missed nothing.

Turtle was growing out of a soft rock.
He put forth his head strangely,
as if the shell yawned and threw out its legs.

He had pulled the world from the dark mirrors of his shell,
from a dark smoke-hole in the middle of himself.

First he painted the sky,
finished it with a bone scraper.
Then he stretched out the roofing of the night,
and covered it with a moisture of starlight.

Now, as if dreaming, he kept closing his eyes.
He held the lids perfectly shut.

Turtle thought he had made the world up,
chipping and chipping with an old bone chisel.
He reminds me of my sister,
of our tent-village, pitched on a narrow ledge
above the Deer Creek river.

Ishi was the Indian, the last of his tribe, who appeared in the town of
Oroville, California, in 1911. His people had lived a life of concealment for
twelve years in the foothills above the town. He was befriended by the
anthropologist Alfred Kroeber, who took him to live in the Museum of
Anthropology at Berkeley.

SILENCE

George Ella Lyon

I speak of silence
of what Schaffhausen taught me
of what I learned from its river
Rhin, Reno, Rhein.

We lived on the border: two
homelands, three languages.
Snow whirled, all its names
frozen thick on our tongues.

Words peeled from the world,
labels from a jar in water.
I beheld the clean vessel.
Silence fell with the light

that danced on the broken river.
Our thin voices glistened.
A scrap of tune from a mouth harp
drifting off on the wind.

Brot, panne, pain:
a mute hand slices.
Mund, bouche, bocca:
the hungry open wide.

GUATEMALA, YOUR NAME

Carmen Matute

to Luis Alfredo Arango

For a long time
I have loved the things of my land:
its jugs
its Chinautla doves
little marimbas of *tecomates*
and big marimbas that come in pairs.
The endless list
of objects
that come from the miraculous hands
of my people:
the *huipiles* of Nebaj
of Cobán
of San Antonio Aguascalientes
or any sad little town.
I also love the poetry captured
in its bowls
its unforgettable shawls
its poor whistles
for clay children
its ceramic butterflies, fruits, birds
its cups and rattles
paint on the round heads of gourds
and the terrible masks
        of the totem animal
        of the shaman
and the beautiful mask of Tecún.

Why go on?
The truth is

I never mentioned
Guatemala in my poems.
How would it fit with its infinite throngs of Indians . . .
But today
Juan came to tell me
in his broken Spanish
that his little Catalino
has been coughing up blood
and I have to shout
that rage and shame
pelted my face
like a rain of stones
and my tongue became a rag in my mouth
when I tried to repeat the wounded
sweet name
of my country.

Translated from the Spanish
by Jo Anne Engelbert

SKULL-LIGHT

Medbh McGuckian

Think of certain inexplicable deaths
as sullied translucent patches on sea,
the sky a stagnant pool. The river
of women wash down their walls
with milk of lime and household starch
for All Saints sideways on purpose now.

I make my Easter walking between the graves,
head high in the air, and seem to be losing him
twice over, though I am far more truly dead,
fastened like a limpet to this strip of land.

The real look is creeping back into his eyes,
eyes I feared to read, that nailed or burned
the words to my lips, and made of his death
with their sudden flaming up a perfect end.

That strange current he gave forth,
as though a beloved red from the topmost
part of evening, a scarce-born animal
in spices, that frozen light
too intense for even the smallest shadow —
what morning, like a sleeve too wide,
without costing much, can be breaking in me?

QUILT OF RIGHTS

Sandra McPherson

Yes, I do see many of us afraid of scraps,
afraid of their big design.
But once, every quilter knew she had a right
to color and shape, even if she believed in
no known meaning of *pretty*.

It is that maker whom I ask to teach me.

In the Muskogee Flea Market this soul's claim
to color passes to anyone.
She built cloth skylights
and for a while trusted herself
to fit just blue ones,
clear around a weather of small forms—
bird's eyes, pollen.
But then she guessed her right to sunny windows;
she colored her way to coral panes;
and finally directed all her vistas
to be plaid: plaid elms, plaid storm,
all shoppers and all dogs
tartan and clashing
as was her right.

No shadings between the frenzied and the cool.

But listen, I tell my rocky soul:
the normality of this—.
For it is not done with moods.
It is given with a right to color.

SNAFU

Jim Wayne Miller

When vandals topple stones in the cemetery,
remember, Alexandria's great library

incurred an ignorant Muslim general's wrath
and fueled the furnaces of the public bath.

The curious carve their initials on beached whales;
Turks once quartered horses in cathedrals.

Recall this when an oil spill rides a river's tide,
or an unctuous preacher descends a waterslide;

when tear gas stings old streets, rising even
over the spot where Muhammad ascended to heaven,

and Palestinian children turn, and run, as a
tank rumbles into the Via Dolorosa.

THE NEW STOVE

Maureen Morehead

There are things my husband doesn't know.
He doesn't know I weigh 123 pounds,
that the new stove makes me nervous,
that when I was a teenager, I was anorexic,
though I have told him this.
I'm not sure he knows
that I'm the tooth fairy.
My children suspect. They hear things at school.
I want to explain this:
the air in the room was starched,
and when we were there, it was not like school
with its green walls and talk and getting
things right. We were neither pithing frogs,
nor labeling their parts, nor translating Caesar,
nor turning, like Persephone, to our boyfriends,
nor reeling in the dark, slow-motion
of reproducing cells,
and though we were there,
and the walls were white,
and we sat in a circle,
and I was there,
I was actually in the restroom
inventing the lines of my cheekbones with red.
I want to say: I was a child. Listen, I'm better.
That the new stove is nice, a good color,
that I will cook things on it, and eat them,
and keep my family healthy,
but sometimes I want to place pots of African violets
on its clean, new burners,
and I want my husband to ask me, where do you go
when I wake in the night and notice you are missing?

WOMAN, EMBRACING TREE

Adrian Oktenberg

You go quietly, and I know where
you are going. I followed you once,
greedy as any lover.
To the woods, to find the white birch
split five ways at the ground, the tree
you think is a secret, that holds your secrets,
like Shiva, in its numerous arms.

I saw you stand,
face to face as a friend would,
but at a slight distance, with respect.
Then you stepped forward
in a measured way, as if
at a ceremony,
held out your arms,
embraced the white birch,
cheek on bark, coolly resting.
Birch bent to you, listening.
You said a few words, held
the tree in your arms for a moment,
stepped back shyly.

I know, you don't have to tell me.
I myself once had a high pasture,
and then a river, many years ago.

Animal Catechism

Olga Orozco

We are hard fragments torn from heaven's reverse,
chunks like insoluble rubble
turned toward this wall where the flight of reality is inscribed,
chilling white bite of banishment.
Suspended in the middle of the landslide because of error,
we stand up against the hostage's miserable condition,
with our flank worn down by the sand's friction
   and chance's blow, exposed
beneath the precarious sun that maybe today will go out,
   won't rise tomorrow.
We have neither the mark of predestination
   nor the vestiges of the first light;
we don't even know what sigh breathes us in and out.
We scarcely know the taste of thirst, the manner of penetrating
   the fog, this dizzying substance in search of escape—
these speak of some place where mutilated visions are completed,
where God is completed.
Ah to discover the hidden and unthinkable image
   of the reflection,
the secret word, the lost good,
the other half that was always a cloud unreachable from solitude
and is all the beauty that binds us in its plot and remakes us,
an eternal glance like a lake in which to submerge love
   in its insomniac version,
in its golden surprise!
But there's no one to see the glimmer of a single crack
   to slip through.
Never with this life that can't go and come,
that reduces the hours and wavers against the wind,
that takes refuge and flickers like a flame stiff with cold
   when death appears.

Never with this body where the universe always stumbles.
It will remain encrusted in this wall.
It will be more opaque than a boulder gnawed by the rain
   till the last judgment.

And will this body be of use for surviving in the beyond,
inept and dethroned monarch, fragile obligatory deserter,
rescued again from its nothingness, from the depths
   of a misty landfill?
Or will it be simply like rubbish that is thrown away
   and forgotten?
No, this body can't be only for entering and leaving.
I reclaim my eyes that watched Etna beneath the embers
   of other eyes:
I beg for this skin with which I fall to the bottom
   of each precipice:
I plead for the hands that searched,
   for the feet that got lost,
I appeal even for the mourning of my blood and the ice
   of my bones.
Even though there is no rest, or permanence, or wisdom,
I defend my place:
this humble dwelling where my fathomless soul is folded,
where it immolates its shadows
and leaves.

Translated from the Spanish
by Mary Crow

The Evening News
(A letter to Nina Simone)

Brenda Marie Osbey

a wail
a whoop
a line brought back from nowhere.
deep violet of memory,
stored up against hard times' coming.
we were righteous then,
experienced in things we had not seen
but always knew
would pass this way.

we had righteousness on our side.

they say you stood before a small audience in new orleans
    last year and abused them for their smallness.
not just their numbers
but their looks.
their soulless way of sitting
and waiting to be entertained.
they told me how you stood there and cursed them good.
told me how they took it
for the sake
of all they used to be so long ago they never could forget.
could only say like the old folk, when cornered perhaps,
said "*i disremember.*"

i asked them what you wore.

i remembered the years i struggled with the very private fear
that i would remain a child forever
and miss all that was major in our one moment of glory.
even a child knows there is one such moment.
one.
even i had sense enough to see you and not weep.
even a child then understood the words
"sister"
"brother"
"people"
"power"

and anyone could see we were all the evening news.

and hear you sing—
at least that was what they called it.
it was my best girlfriend's sister
who came up on us closed off in her bedroom
laughing over her cosmetics, her jewelry, her sex, her t.v.
and instead of sending us out
leaned there in the doorway and smiled,
"you two know so much,
want to be so grown and everything,
need to quit all that giggling
and learn to listen to nina."
that was late autumn.
aletha came into her own bedroom and sat between us on
        the bed.
she turned up the volume
but did not change the station.
we watched her and her college friends
in dashikis and afros
on the evening news.

that year marceline and i listened close

to the lyrics and the ways
the easy breaths and breathless lines
the underground silences
of you and roberta.
we argued and sassed,
slapped hands on our hips at the slightest provocation,
and learned when and when not to apologize for it.
two brown girls acting out,
mothers looking out over our heads that way they had then
whenever we went so far we did not need to be told.
we gave our telephone numbers to those boys
with the hippest walks
the better grade of afro
the deep-changing voices,
and we never took their calls.
we danced the sophisticated sissy
the thing
the shake
the go-on
the soul strut.
we counted our girlfriends,
"soul sister number 1"
"soul sister number 2."
marceline learned to cornrow
and i braided my older brother's bush each night
we were too much and we knew it.
we thought we understood it all.

deep violet
deep violet

but that was years ago.
and you were in your glory then.

then,
while i was still younger than i knew or admitted,
and studying in south of france,

i danced four nights out of five and all weekend,
my arms on the hips or shoulders
of some wiry brother from cameroun or ivory coast
senegal, algeria, panama, martinique,
one of only six or seven young black women at university
among the dozens and dozens of dark men who circled us
weaving their weightless cloth
their heavy guard.
escorted when i would have been alone
fed when i had no hunger
driven when i lacked a destination
protected from the mere possibility of danger —
and danger to them
we knew
meant "frenchmen/
whitemen" —
courted and cosseted
and danced into sleeplessness.
*"you will be old one day, sister.
then, you will sleep fine."*
but their hearts,
the dark wiry hearts of the brothers,
were in the right places.

the foolish ones said
"you are like women of my country"
and feigned weaknesses no one would believe
they ever even remotely had known.
and often enough
had the immediate good sense
to laugh at themselves
and grin at the rest of us.
the others did something like waiting,
danced endlessly,
and at the end of an evening said
"i have this sister,

this nina.
play some for my sister here, man.
man, get up and put on that nina simone."
and we sat in the silence in the dark
as one found the shiny vinyl
and put the needle to the darker groove.
we sat choked with roman cigarettes
too much dancing
too much good food.
we sat listening and did not touch.
we looked at one another's hands
and read recognition there.
one day we would be old.
we would sleep
and no longer know one another.
we sat into the night
until we grew hungry again and sick from the stale air.
we listened
we wailed
we did not touch
or bow down our heads.

and that is the meaning
of the word *expatriate.*

if you live right
if you live right
if you live right

but what has living done for you?

i heard your voice
over the radio late one night in cambridge
telling how you never meant to sing.
whoever interviewed you hardly said a word.

he asked his questions
and you took your time.
you breathed long breaths between phrases,
your speaking voice lighter
and less lived in than i remembered.
you sang a line or two
and talked about your "life."
i asked my question
directly into the speaker —
"what the hell did living do for you, girl?"
i sat on the floor and drank my coffee.
i paced the carpet between your pauses.
i pulled my nightdress up in both hands and danced.
but i got no satisfaction that night.
and, for what it matters,
heaven did not come to me either.

don't talk to me about soul.
don't tell me about *no* damned soul.
years and years and years
of *all night long*
and-a where are you
and making time and doing right.
expatriate years.
years, woman, years.
where *were* you?

and then you sang "Fodder on My Wings"
with not a note of holy in your voice,
and what could i do?
a young woman,
i put myself to bed.

it was the following year
that you cursed them down in new orleans.
dragged for them like muddy water.

i listened to the story on the telephone
or looked into the faces i came on in the streets.
"what"
i asked them
"did she wear?"
and do you think they could tell me?
all i asked the people
was *what did the woman have on?*

and what about it?
if your country's full of lies
if your man leaves you
if your lover dies
if you lose your ground and there is no higher ground
if your people leave you
if you *got* no people
if your pride is hurting
if you got no pride, no soul
if you are living in danger
if you are living in mississippi, baltimore, detroit
if you walk right, talk right, pray right
if you don't bow down
if you hungry
if you old
if you just don't know

please
please
outside-a you there is no/
place to/ go
these are the expatriate years, these.
what is left.

the people dragged their sorry asses out to see you
and you cursed them

you looked out into their faces, those you could see
and accused them
you called them down for all those years.
you sang the songs you sang when you were younger

and you made them pay.

and then
deep violet
and a longer time no one will speak of.

dear nina,
i want to say to you how we did not mean it
how we did not mean to give you up
to let you go off alone that way.
i want to say how we were a younger people, all of us.
but none of it is true.
we used you
and we tossed what we could not use to the whites
and they were glad to get it.
we tossed you out into such danger
and closed our eyes and ears to what was to become of you
in those years—
deep
deep violet—
and worst of all
we did not even say your name.
we ate you like good hot bread
fresh from the table of an older woman
and then we tossed the rest out for the scavengers.
does it matter?
does it matter when and how we did it to you?
does it matter we got no righteousness from it?
that we felt no shame?
does it matter we took all good things in excess then,

and then again?
not only you
but all things?
does it matter we sometimes return to you now,
in the back rooms of childhood friends,
forgiven lovers?
does it matter this is no gift or tribute or right or holy thing
but just a kind of telling
a chronicle to play back
against those images that never quite made it
to the evening news?

how cursed,
how sorry a mess of people can we be, nina
when outside-a you
there is no place
to go?

Lyrics — The line "heaven did not come to me either" is based on the song "If You Live Right (Heaven Belongs To You)" by Nina Simone.

REDEMPTION SONGS

Eric Pankey

The story goes that Seth returned
to Eden in search of a branch
from the tree of life. I believe
the angel was so moved by his plea
that the angel opened the gate
and not only offered a branch
but cut it with his fiery sword.
What Seth heard was the sound of sap
sing out as it boiled and sealed
the wound. And although it lasted
just that moment, and around him
he could witness paradise,
it was the singing of that branch
he would remember when he found
himself back with his people, cold
and tired from his long journey.
As they huddled around the branch
admiring the delicate white
of the petals, the red streaked throat
disappearing into green wood,
as they cut open the ripe fruit
and pulled away the flesh to find
a seed stone as hard and small as
a newborn's fist, he did not tell
them where to plant it. He did not
taste the moist fruit as they passed it,
some commenting on its sweetness,
some on its bitterness, its taste of salt.
He sat and watched the fire he'd built.
He watched his children asleep there

by the flames. And in their breathing
and the sound of the damp wood's
whine, he heard something of the song.
If he could only hear it once again.
If it were a song he'd sung each day
of his life it might have saved him.
When one child woke crying from dreams,
he picked her up and slowly rocked her.
He hummed what he could remember
of a song his mother had sung.
The simple music served its purpose.

WILLOW

Suzanne Paola

The Greeks would have called it a woman, stooping
over her bath, forever on the verge
of being clean. Bending low, spreading
silver hair, the sure virgin.
To those gods, every virgin
was a riddle, life sprang so riotously
from their bodies. How they needed
to bring all things into bloom! One
approached her in her bath, for the warmth
and marble of her skin, and the water
opening, ready to take
what denied itself to a god. But a rage
burns in the made world
against what a god needs. The moon,
turning its sutured face, pitied the girl
who found treachery in beauty,
in flesh. Remade her as a tree.
Caught there, neither damned
nor clean. And the god? He declared that nothing,
not even fall, would bare her again.
So she sits quiet, silver-green, while trees
riot, brick, burgundy and gold. Leaves
flap wildly and fall. Everything
so bloodied, so free! She has become
like the gods, still, and always
suspended above love or water,
where the soul loses itself. Always
envying drowning, that freedom.

TO A DAUGHTER LEAVING HOME

Linda Pastan

When I taught you
at eight to ride
a bicycle, loping along
beside you
as you wobbled away
on two round wheels,
my own mouth rounding
in surprise when you pulled
ahead down the curved
path of the park,
I kept waiting
for the thud
of your crash as I
sprinted to catch up,
while you grew
smaller, more breakable
with distance,
pumping, pumping
for your life, screaming
with laughter,
the hair flapping
behind you like a
handkerchief waving
goodbye.

DEAD WATERS

Marge Piercy

At Aigues Mortes the dog was a practiced beggar.
He patrolled not the big lot where busses disgorge
but a small seaward lot near the private quarter.

We ate our picnic lunch, gazing at the ramparts.
He honed his longing stare on us till we tossed
bits of sausage he caught deftly and bolted.

Finally we threw him a baguette, whole and slightly
stale, thinking he would leave it, teasing him.
But his ears rose as if he heard a fine clear

high note our ears could not reach. He caught the loaf.
He laid it down to examine and then he seized it,
tossed his head smartly and set off at a rapid trot,

the prized baguette in his teeth. Other picnickers called
to him, we tossed after him a bit of sausage, but
he could not be lured back. Off he went in a straight

line at the ramparts and then all along them
to the far gate when he headed in and ran home,
never pausing under the white fish eye of the steamed sun.

A whole loaf of bread. What did that mean to him?
The thing humans never give him? Therefore precious?
Or simply something entire, seamless, perfect for once.

THE DREAM OF SALT

Reynolds Price

I'm waiting for Jesus in a room built of salt,
I have an appointment; he's bound to appear.
But I stand now, studying the white walls round me —
Twenty feet high from a circular floor
And sheered in perfect hard-lined planes.
No one waits with me; I'm forced to stand
(No bench in sight). I'm calm, convinced
My wait will yield uncounted good.
I think one thought continually —
"Don't weep. One tear would melt this room."
Happiness floods me and I pour great tears.

SARAH SHAWCROSS
(1919-1953)

James Reiss

Her first published short story, "Dear Tolstoy,"
  ends with its skewed point of view
focused on the wheels of a Broadway local.

  After splitting from her loverboy husband
she moved from the Upper West Side
  & wrote her best-seller, *Salt Water,*

holed up in an unheated loft overlooking
  a switchyard with so many boxcars
she could hear them screak as they lumbered

  through her sleep. Though she went to bed
with a woman who was a guitarist,
  though they took in twin infants & lived

like royalty in Cuba on her royalties
  three years before her lymphoma,
at heart she was Depression kid

  whose prose rumbled like a locomotive
through landlocked enclaves—Muncie, Decatur—
  en route to a longshoremen's port city.

GOODBYE TO ROBERT GRAVES
(1895-1985)

Natasha Saje

Not twisted
like Eliot,
wired like Pound, or
pinched like Auden—
and you lived longer
than any of them.

Still, women jumped out of windows
with you. A full life:
a wife who wouldn't take your name,
not even to divorce you, and a mistress
who wouldn't make love.

I met you once, tall and rakish
in a black hat, leaning
on the last wife. In a haze,
you winked at me, a would-be
muse, a woman.

You think of us
like missing books, you can't remember
whom you lent us to.
Someday we'll turn up—
with your name on the flyleaf.

AVEC AMOUR

Robyn Selman

There never was a war that was inward.
MARIANNE MOORE

1

The first time I entered France, not by storm
but in a storm, I was met by uniformed

gendarmes with anxious-looking M-16s
shouldered on baby-faced intensity—

the same look I wore on my own young face—
my life, too, was a loaded gun, misplaced.

This was Paris in the sober eighties.
I'd come by boat from Dover in what we

at home call a nor'easter, to Calais,
shipwrecked hair in a Channel-knotted braid,

my Levi's salted stiff with water, my books:
on Vita's and Violet's sisterhood,

another on female orgasms, were
soaked to twice their size, swollen metaphors.

2

Soaked through like a swollen metaphor,
I'd come with someone I don't remember.

I no longer know her name or her hopes
but we kept each other company on the boat,

then the train, in the dismal, droning rain,
and in the gray room where we were detained

by overeager customs inspectors
who frisked me, my duffel bag, and guitar

case. In case of what? Hash? I didn't know
French, and what's worse, there were traces of smoke:

twigs, seeds, papers. They were after weapons
I wasn't carrying, but would have been

had it been the forties, and they Vichy.
I'd have been a Jew with an M-16.

3

I felt like a Jew with her M-16.
After hours (years) of hard questioning,

we were freed and the ardent rain stopped screaming.
We checked into a pension run by

a thin man and his even thinner wife.
Bolted in like refugees, by nine they'd locked up tight.

I was running from Steve, whom I'd left behind
at Kennedy. Really, it had been he

who had long before abandoned me.
Then, I hid. He had male lovers by thirteen.

He'd say he had to do family errands,
but by dinner he'd come around again

with hickies his mother thought came from me.
With the purple marks he also brought a twenty.

4

With the purple marks he brought a twenty
we'd spend on a dime bag and Burger King.

He didn't eat. Instead he got up a dozen times
for mustard, ketchup, ice, another drink.

Licking the salt off the damp, limp fries,
my briny predicament crystallized.

He'd been blowing johns in Fort Lauderdale.
I reasoned that impersonal sex paid well.

Thirsty from the salt, tired of sex talk,
we made out in his van, but always stopped

short, his half-cocked cock sheltered in his pants,
my crotch disarmed by my lack of interest.

The twenty spent, the rendezvous could end.
We tired of picking names for unborn children.

5

Give the imaginary name, Diane,
to my quiet, straight traveling companion.

Give her the understanding she lacked when
she realized that I'd gone to find the kind

of company she wasn't interested
in. We lasted two nights in the same bed.

When she figured out who I was, she left.
I wondered what I had said, then didn't,

then rode down the Boulevard St. Germain
where women glided down the avenue, arms

around each other's waists or hand in hand.
I thought I had died and gone to heaven,

not realizing what I'd seen was simply fashion.
Touching meant much more, or less, where I'd been.

6

Touching meant much more, or less, where I'd been.
But on the bus I thought I felt something

touch my backside. I thought it was an armrest,
an umbrella, grocery sacks that were set

in the aisle. Convinced it was harmless—
a bottle of lemon or orange citrus,

a roast, baguette, a protruding fennel—
I rode with the small pain and I smiled.

Two stops later he grabbed my breasts,
as he released my ass from his five-mile grasp.

I looked around for help that didn't come,
and said one of the French words I knew: *cochon*!

I read in bed through the rest of the trip
and the next time I entered France equipped.

7

Equipped, in love, two Jews with valid documents,
both post-Stonewall smart, one generation apart.

Only one, it turned out, had been liberated.
We loved, we laughed, we couldn't make it

last. I couldn't commit in French or English.
Instead, we lasted as passionate correspondents

who wrote through the recent maelstrom that cost you
your right breast. (The one I kissed when I kissed you.)

Now you and I fight this last late-century war—
not with language, self-censorship or pride,

Nazis, each other, or anti-Semites—
but against cells gone to tumors, gone to knives.

I enter France in a mnemonic storm tonight.
Never, though, to lose you a second time.

BACKCOUNTRY

Charles Semones

Foul as a dog's breath in July,
this spell of falling weather will not do.
The know-it-all on the eleven o'clock news
said it's apt to drop to five below tonight.
Somebody left the north door open. That's
a settled fact. My sinuses are throbbing.
Something I cannot give a name to bothers me.
The radio is tuned to all-night classics —
Brahms a few minutes back. Barber at the moment.
My coffee's getting cold in the souvenir mug
I bought on a trip to Biloxi two summers ago.
There's not another soul for miles around
who's up this late. Just me and that fellow
spinning records on the radio. Jesus Christ,
how long have I been by myself now? I know —
but I do not want to know. It gripes me.
My closest neighbors, a good half-mile away,
have seen fifty-odd winters come and go together.
That counts for something. I forget exactly what.
And if I could remember, what good would it do me?
"The sky's clear as a bell," my father used to say.
And tonight it is. The North Star's bell-tongue cold.
(Speaking of my father, I can almost see him
coming from the lambing barn—his lantern's glow
doing a zigzag dance above the hard-packed snow.
That's over now. He's gone. My mother too.)
I'm alone in this grim farmhouse I was born in,
got a whole half-dollar on my birthdays in,
measured my cock, fretted over its growing in . . .
(They say that somewhere in this world

I've got a half-grown son. Whoever took him from me,
I do not forgive. Not tonight. Not ever.)
This mean season will moderate and pass.
Snow will melt, ooze underground, and push up iris
out by the fieldstone chimney where years ago,
my mother stood in her best print dress
and let me take her picture in the last good light.
What if summer comes back with the virgin-smell
of new-mown hay, plushier than heaven's carpet
that angels sink clean down to their knees in?
October will happen again with its dream of ripe
persimmons, keeper pears, and winter crooknecks.
That much is certain. What is not so certain
is whether we stay or go — and how we manage either.
Some folks never die here: they get crotchety and old.
They look toward every fresh-dug grave with sad envy—
dreading the slow, insidious snake-crawl of new cold.

SMALL TALK

Aleda Shirley

The house you grew up in, the diamond
where you played baseball, the front porch where you
first kissed a girl — you show me these things
and ask to see some place I've lived, any
place, a window in a white frame house
that was mine, a tree I might have climbed

as a child. We drive through the park, over
the bridge you've driven across every day
of your life and dusk falls so fast that for a moment
I think it's rain. In bed when the lights
are off and one of us can't sleep, you whisper
show me and I touch myself and remember an icestorm

in the south, school cancelled for a week, mugs
of tomato soup. I touch your leg with mine
and think of the woman who slept away
all the summers of my childhood, the woman who died
when I was a baby and left me alone
with the man who made maps and followed weather

from continent to continent. If only we could
choose our parents: I would have chosen
the one who gardened on weekends and looked after
his invalid wife, rubbing the blue veins
in her wrist with a cool cloth. I heard him
singing, late at night. *Like this*, I tell you

and feel your breath on my hair, two fingers
running down my spine; I remember poison ivy
growing up the chimney, and white iris—
there must have been a garden. If only we could

choose our gifts: I would have done better
than folding the paper sailboat on the grey rug,

covering my face with your hands, and offered
something glittering, like what you showed me: the moon
following the curve of the bridge into another state.

In Memoriam

Dennis Silk

AFTER UNGARETTI

He was named
Mohammed Sceab

descendant
of emirs of nomads
suicide
because he had no country

loved France
and changed his name
was Marcel
and never French

no longer knew
cushions of his own tent
where, sipping coffee,
they listen to a singsong Koran

didn't know
to free
the song
of his dispersion

I together
with the hotel proprietress
of number 5 rue des Carmes Paris

accompanied
him down a descending alley

He lies
in the cemetery

at Ivry
suburb with its persistent look
of a departing fair

Maybe I
alone know
that he lived

LIES

Eva Skrande

I was a baby born in the arms of a tree.
I had no grandmother, not even
a father or mother.
The few caps I wore, I threw
into a headless river.

I was a boat born without food or wine.
I swam amongst the flotsam of stars.
I had only four fingers

to hold the moon.

I was a window, a church,
an old pair of shoes, an owl in the martyrdom
of night.

I became a flower.
I had one ear to listen for enemies.

I became a song.
I became a heart, lucky and green.

I became a liar.
I rewrote my past.
On the last page of my life
I lulled the wind to sleep
in my arms.

ENTRY

Woodridge Spears

It was the wind rattling a shutter,
It was winter sending a letter.

Upon the clean-swept floor there came
A grain, a speck, the dust of a name.

Into the clean-swept room at night
There came a flicker, a sudden blue light.

A flicker sudden upon a frame,
And never the blue light of a flame.

A small light only on wall and floor,
And passing then, and seen no more.

And the wintry dark was the matter
Again, the wind rattling a shutter.

It was winter sending a letter,
As though somebody's light might enter.

APPLES IN THE WELL

James Still

When a tree shed apples in my well
You were hired to clean it out—
You with the shoulders round enough
To reach sunken pail, scoop crayfish mud,
Clear claws of a mole, a length of chain
From my drinking water.

You who were hired to clean my well
Drowned at last in other depths,
In another year, at a later season,
Where convexity of figure did not count.
You bobbed like an apple in familiarity,
In an element you shared somewhat already.

METAMORPHOSIS

Ruth Stone

One day you wake up and you have a new face.
What's this, you say
in the harsh Kosher manner
of your mother-in-law in a high-class restaurant.

Although your hair is titian red
and not blue rinse like hers —
she always sent whatever it was back —
No matter how many times you look in the mirror
you can't make it go away.

So this is it.
All those women
you thanked god you didn't look like
have surfaced from caves in your cells
where they have been waiting for years
to gather you into their coven.

And now you remember her bitterness.
Too much salt, burned edges;
it was never good enough.

GRAVEYARD QUILT

Catherine Sutton

*Made by Elizabeth Mitchell
Lewis Co., Kentucky, circa 1839*

For months I pieced that quilt.
I tore my own clothes
for brown cloth.
The square print graveyard in the center
holds my sons' white coffins
alone as I left them
in the Ohio earth.
Outside the picket fence border,
where we still live,
I lay out thirteen more coffins—
one for each of us alive,
fine with embroidered names.

Just a few stitches hold me here;
I'll never know everything
that quilt could say about me.
I sewed through all my grief
then put it on the bed
and left the room.

When I was a girl
they bred us to the needle
and taught us to live
on the narrow seams of scraps.
Women bragged on what
they made for nothing.

Winter nights, I sleep beneath my sons.

THE LONE PEDESTRIAN

May Swenson

I wander out, the lone pedestrian
in Lafayette, and walk the west
side of the Wabash past the Sunday
houses. Don't know where you are,
hope *not* to meet you—but
you're snowing in my mind. "About
that telegram you sent: I thought
the initials meant from Bobby K.
Wired back 'Thank you.' They
typed it 'Fuck you,' and now he's
sore at me. See how you screw up
all the time—though with the best
intentions?" You laugh, and I
congratulate myself: "The Smothers
Brothers ought to get me to write
their gags." I see you pull
the word-strips off like sunburned
skin, standing in your ski coat in
my living room—you couldn't get it
off, the zipper was jammed—I didn't
offer to help. I had a toothache,
and here you'd come, a day early and
without phoning first, butting at
my door. You walk, head down, like
a sun-stunned bull, did you know?
You left the Volks as usual turned on
at the curb, shoved a bag of Key limes
at me, *pretending* you weren't coming
in, when you knew damn well I'd
invite you—would *have* to, wouldn't I?

You force, by backing up, "the shaft,"
as you call it, to follow—then lean
on it moving in, so *it* moves in—did
you know? While I—I'm *not* the *pie*—
maybe the blanketed horse—Yes, I'm
self-saving, wrap myself in
indifference. When weak, I'm scared—
that's why I act like that. You
scare me. Let me go on. Maybe explain.
It's snowing. Hard. I'm back in the
house. Brought back some candles,
transistor batteries, carton of cigs.
The matches you gave me I still have—
pretty colors without ads. You're
snowing in my mind. While walking
home: "It's that we find ourselves doing
things we'd never do sends us crazy.
Finding we can be makes us come to it.
Which goes for both—and everyone."
Right now, standing at the screen
door: "Somehow it's what I admire
you for I hate you for"—peering
through the snow—A car goes by slow,
windows blinded, groping—a woman
driver—then a Volks—a boy—shoots
by, ignoring the thickening, slick danger—
snow. I know you'd come like that,
in a quick skid, you were coming—
mount my porch, maybe, crash through
my caution and my living room.
That's in my mind, where I admire how
you are. My actuality can't take you.
It says: "Come. Stay." At the same
time it says: "Stay afar."

At this minute, where could you be?
In hospital, on the road, on the ski-

slope, in a sweatroom at French Lick,
or under water, eye-to-eye with sharks?
You're barracuda, too—you know—
You know that I'm scared of you. It's
that gun you've got, in the glove, and
bright pellets you strung through
your nail-bitten hands once, sitting in
the car—same hands that knit
the sox, the Valentine heart on the
toe, you began to give me two days
ago—You snow me all the time, Big
Bragger, Big Cry Baby—on the phone
panting like a junkie caught without—
You manipulate, or confabulate—you're
either nuts or had your conscience
lopped—you're LSD'd, S-M, AC/DC—
I don't know—could be all that, so what, that's
not it—It's "Is that a gun in your
pocket, or are you glad to see me?"
Made me laugh so hard. But that
gun's real—and the answer's "Yes—
and No." You're the one who tore my
doorknob off Friday night—Right?
Enraged that I wouldn't let you in.
I was out that time—at the movie—
I'd told you so. So where are you
now? In jail? At the Redhead's? On
the squash court? Or bugging Mother
in that house of clocks in Washington?
"What do *you* care?" I hear you sneer.
I'm glad I don't know, I guess. I
can't help it, being me, anymore than
you can quit being you. Can you? I
hope you can't quit. . . being. That's
your biggest scare—your way to
score big, isn't it? But it scares
you, too. I hope it does. Hope you'll

scare yourself to sense. To sense,
to feel—to feel the human in you—
to love it—love your *self*, first,
foremost—let your body take care—
of you in it—the you that loves.

I almost called that cop named King
you know. Took his number along to
the movie Friday, just in case.
You're ugly when angry, Nasty Mouth.
Angry, when sick, I know—but sick
because self-beaten, bruised, starved,
strafed, driven on, tired out, shot
down. Snow's deep blue now. Twilight
out the window. It's Sunday night.
"In this nook that opens south. . ."
was Wednesday you came—I'd
started to write—and brought me limes.
When I wouldn't play the game the way,
somewhere in your head since Florida,
you thought I would, and ought—that
head that cannot dream if, as you say,
it never sleeps—"The head is dead. . . ."
No, that was then—a summer time,
in "Good day, sunshine" weather-blond
head, dazzled grin, on the snapshot
you labeled your "2nd happiest day"—
and I was supposed to say, "What is
the first?"—and didn't, since supposed
to. That head—Goldy Lox—with foolish red cap
on—you holding my foot instead of
hand that night I had toothache—
expecting to make me, weren't you?—
"I can get anyone in the world
interested in me"—You told on
yourself there, you know—and all
that you told about getting dumped

in front of the Waldorf—about faking
it out in the interview at Rutgers—
about "Arne being used to it"—you
freaking out on him—"I'm a little
unreliable once in a while," you
admitted. "But notice my charm, my
cool—I do my dirt with style,"
your cocky chuckle said. You swiping
the air and pacing the rug. You told
on yourself there, Bouncer—over and
over—and when you bounced that
volleyball off the wall so's to barely
miss my head—"that hair" you crow
over and snow me about—"I thought
if I could touch it just one more
time." Before you climb the cliff, I'm
supposed to think. Can't you see you
kissed yourself off, slugged yourself
out, dumped on yourself all that
evening? Hauled away the record player,
threw down Webster's 3rd in its place,
on the bed, like a slab of ice. Christ,
you're funny! Wish I could laugh,
like I used to, two months back. You
made me glad then—crazy glad—
unleashed, MacLeished, I believed you—
Like I said, "I believe everything you
say till I find out different." Well,
I've found out, haven't I? You aced
yourself right out of the game, and
just when it was ripe, you thought, to
run all your way. You've got big cards
—so big you throw them away. I had
my little significant present for you—
Had you got it in N.Y. from R., would
all of it now be different, I wonder?
Maybe, and maybe worse. We might be

snowed in here, tight, trapped, cozy with
that gun you've got between us—me
wasting more of my time than I'm
doing now, with this not-poem, trying
to plough you out of my mind. Snow's
falling on all the squirrels in all
the heavy arms of all the pines out
there, where it's dark. It's yellow
in here. Goldy, you wouldn't take my
gold-wrapped trinket—and I had
Russian Leather for you, too—to make
you—smell so good—And you threw
back my Mother's 25-carat gold ring
along with a nasty misspelled note
making those funny *d's* that you do—
And you threw me gold yarn sox you'd
knitted—that makes 4 pair—with the
mistake you warned me was in one toe—
And threw me 2 basketball tickets clipped
to a sweet note next morning, Thursday,
in my mailbox. Then phoned. I was
still asleep. "Can you give me
breakfast?" I said, "No"—and didn't
thank you for anything—stayed mute
and mum—disconnected—But this was
before I'd been to the mailbox, remember?
You so demanding, so damned awake and
breathless. My tooth hurt, I wasn't up
yet—said "Call me later." You snarled:
"*You* call *me.*" So I didn't. O.K., so
somehow—but how?—how should I know, with
you it was more than a sore tooth?
And after the dentist, and after I'd
been working all day on that mistake-of-
a-piece for the mag for you—you
dumbbunny, diddling with that sycophant
dumbdaddy A., who you say you've thrown

over because you dropped a critical
stitch back there somewhere, made a booboo
with the manipulation switch—and had
it about done and off my neck so I could
think about starting to do what I had
been supposed to do, *my* work, all day—
No, wait a minute, that was the *next*
day, Friday—Thursday I made you take
me to the lecture, but you were late, and
I walked and met you in the Volks—you
were dolled up, net stockings on, band-
aids showing through where you'd banged
yourself on the squash court—By the
way, Tony that night—No, that had to
be Friday—Anyway, he limped, I can
tell you that—You strained a muscle
in his buttock—he could hardly walk
upstairs. I'm laughing now. I'm
laughing! It feels good. Bouncer,
you idiot, you Wild Thing—it's you,
you know, they sing about in Bobby's
voice on the top ten—"With those
initials you could be President."
"I'm gonna be a big man in town. . ."
"I'm gonna make it. . ." I've got you
humming that. I liked the back
of your bully neck in my hand—I
can't stand it if I've been too
mean to you—Have I been? I didn't
mean to. You—last time I saw you,
at the lecture—nodded you out—
and showed how you'd learned one
lesson—you didn't fade, until I
told you that line, did you?—with my, I guess
you thought, disdainful nod. It
wasn't meant to be. I'm just lost—
more or less, like you. Only more—

scared—and hate myself for that.
And when I hate myself I go cold
and stiff, I settle in—into my
self, old horse in blankets armed—
or old stubborn horny turtle.
Remember how you said you shot
at them in The Keys? But didn't hit
any, you said. That's good. And you
are, too. But crazy. And I drive
you. To that. I know. That's why
you and I—can't. "Snowy gull and
sooty crow. . . ." You see? It's late
now. I'm alone. And want to be.
Stopped snowing.

All yesterday was silent. Saturday.
There's more. There's lots more. Have
to stop now. I wish you well. Where
you are. Hear your voice on phone say:
"Good-bye, though." After I said, "I
hope you'll feel. Better." Those words,
if last, were gentle. Where did you
go? After you broke my door-
knob off? I want to, and I don't
want to, know.

THE DIALECTIC OF SNOW
IN THE PHASES OF WONDER

Richard Taylor

At first, who isn't dazzled?
The backyard's drab particulars
revert to elementary dunes,
billows and swags
that lap against the hillside,
a glittering manifesto.
Humped with snow, the dwarf magnolia
dissolves into the ridgeline.
The field beyond is tabula rasa,
a span of untracked innocence.

But purity wears. We find
monotony in the frugal slopes,
a white hyperbole
that deprives as it illuminates.
Whether by inches or the foot,
snow becomes nothing so much
as bland assertion.

What we crave before the day is out
are definition, contrast, thaw—
the renaissance of shadow,
another dawn with landmarks,
earthly smudges, some dark repatriation.

In Memory of a Closed House

Jorge Teillier

My friend dares to play the guitar
that his father left him in his will.
The steps of the dead man echo
through the deserted halls.
A shadow sits down
in front of the unlit hearth.

In the kitchen broken cups,
dirty pans, remain.
Beside the fence,
under scattered drizzle,
silence just arrived
makes friends with the dogs.

In front of the closed door
we shake hands
and we part without looking back.

Translated from the Spanish
by Mary Crow

THE WORLD IS

Richard Tillinghast

The world is a man with big hands
and a mouth full of teeth.
The world is a ton of bricks, a busy signal,
your contempt for my small talk.
It's the crispy lace that hardens
around the egg you fry every morning
sunny side up.

The world is the last week of August,
the fumes that dizzy up into the heat
when you fill your tank
on the way to work late, again.
The world is "Please take a seat over there."
The world is "It'll have to come out."
The world is "Have a nice day."

The world is "What is that peculiar smell?"
The world is the button that popped off,
the watch that stopped, the lump you discover and turn
    on the light.
The world is a full ashtray, the world is that grey look,
the world is the County Coroner of Shelby County.
The world is a cortege of limousines,
an old man edging the grass from around a stone.

The world is "Belfast Says No!," the world is reliable
sources, a loud bang and shattered glass raining down
    on shoppers.
The world is a severed arm in a box of cabbages, "And
    then

the second bomb went off and we didn't know which

way to run." The world is Semtex and black balaclavas
and mouth-to-mouth resuscitation. The world is
car alarms silenced, and a street suddenly empty.

The world is one thousand dead today in the camps.
The world is sixty thousand latrines, the world is
bulldozers pushing bodies and parts of bodies into a
    ditch.
The world is dysentery and cholera,
infected blood, and vomit.
The world is mortality rates, and rape as an instrument of
    war. The world
is a 12-year-old with a Walkman, a can of Coke, and an
    Uzi.

An Unceasing Flow of Tears

Edwina Trentham

The evening paper slaps
the screen. I call the children home,
scan the headlines. Only the little
nightmares change from day to day. I find
them clumped together, lost
on an inside page. Clues sought in Long Island
slaying. Mother and two children.
Outside the fields dapple
gold, dandelions clinging to the last
light. Hundreds of stab wounds.
I cook supper
for the children: fat-flecked
hamburgers chirping
in the oven's heat. Elderly woman surprises
teenage robbers. Soft strawberries
of blood puddle the broiler
pan. Struck on the back
of the head. Sodomized as she lay
dying. I draw the curtains against
the darkness. Soviet writer beaten
last year still can't work. I run
bathwater, listen to the children squabble
in the kitchen. Steam clouds
the mirror, can't be wiped away, fine
drops trickling down the glass
across my eyes. He still
suffers from headaches, causing
an unceasing flow of tears.

X:
FOR PATRICK HENISSE, DEAD OF AIDS, IN MEMORY

Jean Valentine

*I have decorated this banner
to honor my brother. Our parents did
not want his name used publicly.*

—from The AIDS Memorial Quilt

The boatpond, broken off, looks back at the sky.
I remember looking at you, X, this way,
taking in your red hair, your eyes' light, and I miss you
so. I know,
you are you, and real, standing there in the doorway,
whether dead or whether living, real. — Then Y
said, "Who will remember me three years after I die?
What is there for my eye
to read then?"
The lamb should not have given
his wool.
He was so small. At the end, Pat, you were so small.
Playing with a stone
on your bedspread at the edge of the ocean.

AMMA'S RUBY

Reetika Vazirani

Many cringed because Amma gave jewels
to relations according to her whim.
At her sons' weddings she brought each bride
diamonds, reticence, filigree in gold;
and the weddings were long, and women wore tiers
of handstrung pearls and some wore sapphires,
as if Seeta's trail of gems was seen again —
clues dropped from a fleeing chariot
so that the prince, her husband, would follow them.

Amma passed a ruby through my mother to me.
It fits my ring finger, and suitors think I'm engaged.
I'm not. And it's odd because this stone
was found flawed at the markets by Amma's maid
who couldn't trade it for a decent fish.

INVITATION

Cia White

I mean
   to turn up the heat.
I mean
   to run you out.

Patrons, guests:
the cook's gone greedy,
this groaning board
is all for me, the meal
I make myself
in the presence of mine enemies.

Let there be soup.

I mean
   to make a mean soup.

In service I have learned
all about the use of salt
grinding spice
melting marrow out of bone
crushing the swooning sprig of herb
oiling the fingers with its essence
masking the unsavory
to make it look so good
so good for you
so good
   of you
to come last to the table
bearing the ladle
and an ineffable smile.

And let those who have been drinking
    me
clear the hall, go
break another's loaf, or better
make your own,
another Martha's run amok.

I mean
    to be the official
taster and the favorite
who dares it
and I will be the lonely queen.
I will be the widow in the wood
bent at dusk
over the steaming bowl,
broth reduced of tares,
red berries, lowly green
medicinals.
And I'll be Jacob too
I mean
    to enjoy my fragrant portion
though I must put on skins
and stink of the hunt.

I mean
    to make this soup.

Stand off, or swallow
what of it you will,
it will be full of small bones
to catch in the throat
and grit, a stone, the blade
of what serrate leaf
comes to hand.

Somewhere may be others
with tongues tempered like mine
to this heat, and to them

it may be mead:
first, though, it must be mine:
my meal, my meat.

EXILE: JERUSALEM

Ruth Whitman

*Give me a place to stand
and I'll move the world.*
—Archimedes

Spring again. And no place to stand.
Images of street life — buses, beggars,
an old man sleeping on the sidewalk,
an Arab woman squatting among her baskets—
are written in an alphabet I haven't learned,
syllables of meaning in a wordless desert.

Over the dusty hills,
beyond the sappers dismantling the bomb,
beyond the fury of stones,
across the gardens of oranges in this
sacred airless well,
the sea is speaking,

a universal turquoise language
I understand, but can't hear.

Sonya

Marie Sheppard Williams

I went into old
fat Sonya's room
in the nursing home.
Dobre utro, Sonya,
I said and I whipped
back the curtains
to let in the day.

Look, darling, it's
raining, I said.
Her sad eyes stared
at the window and
filled with tears.

It's raining in
Russia too, Sonya.
The rain is the same
rain all over.

               She
rolled her head slowly
from side to side like
a baffled pain-racked
bear. Her eyes said
No. This is not the rain
that falls in Russia.

MOTHER'S DAY

Daisy Zamora

To my children

I don't doubt you would have liked to have had
a pretty mother from a t.v. commercial:
                    with an adorable husband and happy children.
She always looks cheerful—and if she cries some day—
she does it once the lights and cameras have been shut off
and with her face, make-up free.

But because I brought you into the world, I must tell you:
Ever since I was little like you
I yearned to be myself—and for a woman that is difficult—
(even my Guardian Angel renounced caring for me
when he found out).

I cannot assure you that I am very familiar with the path.
I make mistakes many times,
and my life has been rather like a painful voyage
overcoming obstacles, dodging storms,
ignoring spectral sirens inviting me to the past,
without an adequate compass or logbook
to show me the way.

But I advance, I advance clinging to the hope
of some distant harbor
to which—I am sure—you, my children
will arrive someday
—after my shipwreck
has been consummated—.

*Translated from the Spanish
by Celeste Kostopulos-Cooperman*

NOTES ON CONTRIBUTORS

Paula Gunn Allen, a Laguna Pueblo-Sioux-Scottish-Lebanese-American poet and scholar, is perhaps best known for her collection of essays, *The Sacred Hoop: Recovering the Feminine in American Indian Traditions* (Beacon Press) □ Yehuda Amichai is a leading Israeli poet whose collections include *From Man Thou Art, To Man Thou Shalt Return* and *Selected Poems* (Harper & Row). Translator Karen Alkalay-Gut teaches at Tel Aviv University, and her most recent book of poems is titled *Ignorant Armies* (Cross-Cultural Communications) □ Wendell Berry is a farmer, poet, essayist, and novelist. His books include *The Unsettling of America* (Harper & Row) and *The Collected Poems of Wendell Berry* (North Point Press) □ Michael Blumenthal's books of poems include *Sympathetic Magic* (Water Mark) and *Days We Would Rather Know* (Random House). He teaches at Harvard University □ Jorge Luis Borges was the legendary South American polymath, author of numerous books, including *Ficciones, Labyrinths,* and *The Book of Imaginary Beings.* Translator Hardie St. Martin has translated Pablo Neruda's *Memoirs* (Farrar Straus & Giroux) and is the editor of *Roots and Wings: Poetry from Spain 1900-1975* (Harper & Row) □ Diana Brebner's poems have appeared in many Canadian journals. Her first collection, *Radiant Life Forms* (Netherlandic Press), won the 1990 Gerald Lampert Memorial Award □ Lee Ellen Briccetti's poems have appeared widely, and she currently serves as the Executive Director of Poets House in New York City □ Olga Broumas' *Beginning with O* won the 1977 Yale Younger Poets prize. Subsequent collections include *Perpetua* and, with T Begley, *Sappho's Gymnasium* (both from Copper Canyon Press) □ Joseph Bruchac has published poems widely, and collected them in *Near the Mountains: New and Selected Poems* (White Pines Press). For many years, he edited *The Greenfield Review*

☐ Olga Cabral was born in the West Indies, of Portuguese descent, and has published several books of poetry, most recently *The Green Dream* (Contact II Publications) ☐ Ernesto Cardenal has served as the Minister of Culture for Nicaragua, and is the author of several books, among them *With Walker in Nicaragua* (City Lights) and *Apocalypse*. Translator Jonathan Cohen has written widely about Latin American culture, and has translated the works of Cardenal, Oquendo de Amat, and others ☐ Barbara Carey lives in Toronto. She has published several books of poetry, among them *Undressing the Dark, The Year in Pictures,* and *The Ground of Events* ☐ Richard Chess teaches at the University of North Carolina. His poems have been published in *Tikkun, The Missouri Review, Ironwood,* and *New England Review/Bread Loaf Quarterly,* among others ☐ Marilyn Chin was born in Hong Kong and raised in Oregon. Her first book of poems, *Dwarf Bamboo,* was nominated for the Bay Area Book Reviewer's Award. She teaches at San Diego State University ☐ Jennifer Clement belongs to the Tramontane group of poets in Mexico City. She has published poems widely, and collected them in *The Next Stranger* (Ediciones El Tucan de Virginia, Mexico) ☐ Jane Cooper's first book, *The Weather of Six Mornings,* won the Lamont Award of the Academy of American Poets. Her most recent book is *Scaffolding: Selected Poems* (Tilbury House) ☐ Pablo Antonio Cuadra has published many books of poems, including *The Birth of the Sun* (Unicorn Press). Translator Steven F. White is the author of *Culture and Politics in Nicaragua* and *For the Unborn* (poetry), among others ☐ Mark Doty teaches at Sarah Lawrence College. His books of poems include, most recently, *My Alexandria.* He serves as an advisory editor to *The American Voice* ☐ Sue Terry Driskell has published poems in *The Louisville Review, Plainsong, The Greensboro Review,* and in a chapbook, *Turnabout* (Beech Grove Press) ☐ Odysseas Elytis was awarded the 1979 Nobel Prize for literature. "Anoint the Ariston" is from *The Little*

Mariner (Copper Canyon Press), translated by Olga Broumas (see author's note) □ Elaine Equi teaches in New York City, and has published several books of poetry, among them *Surface Tension* and *Voice-Over* (both from Coffee House Press) □ Jan Freeman serves as an editor of Paris Press. Her books of poems include *Hyena* (Cleveland State University Press) and *Autumn Sequence* (Paris Press) □ Tess Gallagher has published several books, among them *Moon Crossing Bridge,* which was selected for the ALA 1993 Notable Books, and she recently received the Lyndhurst Prize for poetry □ Suzanne Gardinier's collection of poems, *The New World* (University of Pittsburgh Press), won the 1992 AWP Award Series. A previous short collection, *Usahn,* was published by Grand Street □ Jane Gentry teaches at the University of Kentucky. She has published poems widely, and recently collected them in *A Garden in Kentucky* (University of Arkansas Press) □ Sarah Gorham is the publisher of Sarabande Books, in Louisville. Her two collections of poems are *Don't Go Back to Sleep* (Galileo Press) and *Tension Zone,* which recently won the Four Way Book Award □ E.J. Graff has published poems in *The Threepenny Review, Ikon,* and *Sojourner,* among many others □ Marilyn Hacker has published many books of poems, among them *Going Back to the River* and *Assumptions* (both from Random House). She is a past editor of *The Kenyon Review* □ James Baker Hall is a photographer and poet. His books include a novel and two collections of poems, *Stopping on the Edge to Wave* (Wesleyan University Press) and *Fast Signing Mute* (Larksur Press) □ Linda Hogan's recent book of poems, *Seeing Through the Sun,* received an American Book Award from the Before Columbus Foundation □ Lynda Hull's poems appeared widely, and her first book, *Ghost Money* (University of Massachusetts Press), won the 1986 Juniper Prize □ Ha Jin has published two books of poetry, *Between Silences* and *Facing Shadows* (both from Hanging Loose Press). He teaches at Emory University in Atlanta □ Myrr Jonason has served as a Peace Corps volunteer in Malaysia, and has published work in Garrett's *Intro 7* and *The Georgia Review,* among others ☐ Brigit Pegeen Kelly's books of poems include *To the Place of Trumpets* (Yale University Press) and *Song* (BOA Editions), which won the 1994 Lamont Poetry Selection of the Academy of American Poets ☐ Jane Kenyon published many books of poems in her lifetime, among them *Let Evening Come* and *The Boat of Quiet Hours* (both from Graywolf Press). She lived with her husband, poet Donald Hall, at Eagle Pond, in New Hampshire ☐ Barbara Kingsolver's poem comes from her collection *Another America/Otro America* (Seal Press). Her novels include *The Bean Trees* and *Pigs in Heaven* (both from Harper & Row) ☐ Yusef Komunyakaa's poems have appeared widely, and have been collected in *Lost in the Bonewheel* (Lynx House Press) and *Copacetic* (Wesleyan University Press). He won the Pulitzer Prize for poetry in 1994 ☐ Natalie Kusz is the author of a memoir, *Road Song* (Farrar Straus & Giroux), and is a recipient of Whiting and Pushcart prizes ☐ James Laughlin was the founder and publisher of New Directions books. His own writings have been collected into many books, among them *Selected Poems 1935-1985* and *The Master of Those Who Know* (both from City Lights) ☐ Dorianne Laux's two books of poems are *Awake* and *What We Carry* (both from BOA Editions) ☐ Li-Young Lee's poem "A Story" is from his first book, *Rose* (BOA Editions). He has also received Whiting and Guggenheim prizes ☐ Ursula LeGuin has published many books, among them *Blue Moon Over Thurman Street* (New Sage Press) and *The Language of the Night: Essays on Fantasy and Science Fiction* (HarperCollins) ☐ Sabra Loomis is a musician and has published poems in *Manhattan Poetry Review, Cincinnati Poetry Review,* and *Violet,* among others. Her first book is *Rose Tree* (Alice James Books) ☐ George Ella Lyon writes children's books, librettos, short fiction and poetry. Recent publications include *Red Rover, Red Rover* (Orchard Books) and *Choices*

(University Press of Kentucky) ☐ Carmen Matute has published two collections of poems, *Circulo Vulnerable* and *Poeta Solo* (both from RIN 78, Guatemala). Translator Jo Anne Engelbert, on a Fulbright research grant, is completing a bilingual anthology of Central American poetry ☐ Medbh McGuckian has published several collections of poems: *The Flower Master, Venus and the Rain,* and *On Ballycastle Beach* (all from Oxford University Press), among them. She is a native of Belfast, Ireland ☐ Sandra McPherson teaches at the University of California, and has published several books of poems, including *Streamers, Patron Happiness,* and *The Year of Our Birth* (all from Ecco Press) ☐ Jim Wayne Miller taught German at Western Kentucky University for many years. His books include *Brier, His Book* and *Newfound* (both from Gnomon Press) ☐ Maureen Morehead has published two books of poems, *In a Yellow Room* and *Our Brother's War* (both from Sulgrave Press). Her poems have appeared in *The Iowa Review* and *American Poetry Review,* among others ☐ Adrian Oktenberg is the founder of Paris Press. She has published poems in *New Letters, The Bennington Review,* and *A Room of One's Own,* among others ☐ Olga Orozco has published more than a dozen books in her native Argentina. Translator Mary Crow has published a book of her own poems, *Borders* (BOA Editions), and other translations ☐ Brenda Marie Osbey has published in *2Plus2* and other journals. Her books include *Ceremony for Minneconjou* (Callaloo Press) and *In These Houses* (Wesleyan University Press) ☐ Eric Pankey directs the writing program at St. Louis University. His first book of poems, *For the New Year* (Atheneum), won the Academy of American Poet's Walt Whitman Award ☐ Suzanne Paola has published poems widely, including *Chelsea, Ironwood,* and *Seneca Review* ☐ Linda Pastan has published several books of poems, among them *The Imperfect Paradise* and *A Fraction of Darkness* (both from Norton) ☐ Marge Piercy is a novelist, essayist and poet. Her books include *Summer*

People (Summit), *Available Light* and *My Mother's Body* (both from Alfred A. Knopf) □ Reynolds Price teaches at Duke University, and has published many books, among them *Private Contentment, Vital Provisions,* and *The Source of Light* (all from Atheneum) □ James Reiss teaches at the University of Dayton, and has published two books of poems, the most recent *The Parable of Fire* (Carnegie-Mellon University Press) □ Natasha Saje's first book, *Red Under the Skin* (University of Pittsburgh Press), won the 1993 Agnes Lynch Starrett Poetry Prize □ Robyn Selman's poems have been published widely. Her first collection, *Directions to My House* (University of Pittsburgh Press), was published in 1995. "Avec Amour" was reprinted in *The Best American Poetry 1995* □ Charles Semones has published in *Wind, Kansas Quarterly, Yellow Silk,* and others. His poem *Homeplace* was recently published by Larkspur Press □ Aleda Shirley's first book of poems, *Chinese Architecture* (University of Georgia Press), won the 1987 Poetry Society of America's Norma Farber First Book Award. She is a visiting writer at the University of Mississippi □ Dennis Silk is a poet, translator and editor living in Jerusalem □ Eva Skrande is a Cuban-American writer and teacher. She has published poems in *The Iowa Review* and *Cutbank,* among others, and in a chapbook, *The Gates of the Somnambulist* (Jeanne Duvall Editions) □ Woodridge Spears taught for many years at Georgetown College, Kentucky. He published three books of poems in his lifetime: *The Feudalist, River Island,* and *Concord* □ James Still teaches at the Hindman Settlement in eastern Kentucky. His many books include *The Wolfpen Poems* (Gnomon Press) and *River of Earth* (University Press of Kentucky) □ Ruth Stone is a long-time teacher and poet. Her many books include *Second-Hand Coat* (David Godine) and *Simplicity* (Paris Press) □ Catherine Sutton is a Kentucky native. She teaches at Bellarmine College in Louisville □ May Swenson published eleven books of poems in her lifetime. "The Lone Pedestrian" comes from the forthcoming book, *The Love*

Poems of May Swenson (Houghton Mifflin) ☐ Richard Taylor teaches at Kentucky State University, and has published a historical novel, *Girty* (Gnomon Press), and a book of poems, *In the Country of Morning Calm* (Larkspur Press) ☐ Jorge Teillier is the author, most recently, of *Para un pueblo fantasma* and *Muertes y Maravillas* (Editorial Universitaria de Chile). Translator Mary Crow teaches at Colorado State University and has published translations of Enrique Lihn, Carmen Orrego, Marco Martos, and Olga Orozco ☐ Richard Tillinghast is the author of five books of poems, most recently *The Stonecutter's Hand* (David Godine). He teaches at the University of Michigan ☐ Edwina Trentham has published poems in *The Nation, The Poetry Miscellany, The Red Fox Review, Embers,* and other journals ☐ Jean Valentine's books include *Home. Deep. Blue: New and Selected Poems* (Alice James Books) and *The Messenger* (Farrar, Straus & Giroux). She lives in New York City ☐ Reetika Vazirani's book of poems, *White Elephants* (Beacon Press), won the Barnard New Women Poet's Prize. She teaches at the University of Virginia ☐ Cia White has taught high school English, and has published poems in *Journal of Kentucky Studies* and *The American Voice,* among others ☐ Ruth Whitman has published poems widely, and collected them in several books, among them *Tamsen Donner: A Woman's Journey* and *Permanent Address, New Poems 1973-1980* (Alice James Books) ☐ Marie Sheppard Williams has published stories in *Hurricane Alice* and *Alaska Quarterly Review,* among others. Her collection of stories is *The Worldwide Church of the Handicapped* (Graywolf Press) ☐ Daisy Zamora is one of Nicaragua's leading poets and human rights activists. Her recent books are *A cada quien la vida,* and, in translation, *Riverbed of Memory.* Translator Celeste Kostopulos-Cooperman has translated the work of many writers, among them Soledad Alvarez, Paz Molina, Mercedes Escolano, and Maria Sanz.

About the Editor

Frederick Smock is the founding editor of *The American Voice*. He is the author of two books of poems, most recently *Gardencourt* (Larkspur Press), and a travel memoir, *This Meadow of Time: A Provence Journal* (Sulgrave Press). His work has appeared in *Poetry, The Iowa Review, American Literary Review,* and many others. In 1995, he received an Al Smith Fellowship in Poetry from the Kentucky Arts Council. Mr. Smock teaches at Bellarmine College.